Destination
2000
Moving The Church Into The 21st Century

Bob Sjogren

This book is dedicated to the unreached Muslims, Buddhists, Hindus, Chinese and Tribal groups of the world. It is hoped that God will use this book to be a catalyst in seeing laborers sent out to start churches among them.

A special thanks goes out to Don Richardson who has trained me in a majority of the material and who continues to be my mentor in my pursuit of knowing the Scriptures.

Also, I wish to give special thanks to Bill Stearns, who so masterfully put the words together in this book; to Dorothy Schulte, who has labored faithfully at the computer; and to my precious mother, who did the final editing.

As you read this book . . .

Each day 37,000 Muslims die and go into a Christ-less eternity.

The majority of them have never had an opportunity to hear what Christ did for them on the cross 2,000 years ago. They live beyond the reach of today's church and there are few trying to minister to them. There is only one missionary for every one million Muslims. More laborers are desperately needed, and that is why FRONTIERS and this book have come into existence.

FRONTIERS exists to see church planting teams with a minumum of six people established to raise up viable churches in the heart of the Muslim world! Each team is custom designed to fit into the geographical and cultural context of its targeted Muslim people group.

Most of the FRONTIERS teams are made up of everday, ordinary people. And most of them at one time never had a clue that God was preparing them to reach Muslims. Many of these team members are on the field in the role of tentmakers, fully aware that God gets greater glory as He uses the weaknesses and dependencies of everday, ordinary people. People like you.

As you read this book, please ask God to show you if He wants you involved in reaching out to Muslims. Maybe you will want to join one of our 59 established teams or form a team from within your church or community after reading this book.

My prayer is that you will want to consider this career direction as you see the tremendous priority our Lord has placed on reaching all nations.

Table of Contents

Introduction

"Detroit 37"

I was once asked to speak at a church conference in Mt. Pleasant, Michigan. At the time I was living in Columbus, Ohio, and I wanted to bring my wife along, so I telephoned and asked for directions.

The person I spoke with said, "Just go north until you hit Detroit, take a left and head toward East Lansing. There, you'll hit a loop. Start out at the bottom of that loop, go to the top, take a right, and that road will take you directly to our church!"

I saw no problems with the directions as I looked at the map.

As we were driving, we began to play the alphabet game to pass the time. Unfortunately, it was the wrong game for me to play because my wife "cheats." You see, her eyesight is better than mine and she'll spot the signs about half a second earlier than I will. Therefore she's way ahead of me in the game.

Yet for those of you who have played the game, you know it isn't that big of a deal, because once you hit the letter "Q", "Q" is the killer. You're either looking for a Quaker State motor oil sign or a Quality Inn sign.

Well, by the time we had passed Detroit and were on our way to East Lansing, Debby was on "Q" and I was on "B"! But it didn't matter. By the time we reached the bottom of that loop, we both were on "Q."

Now, being the competitive person I am, I wanted to beat my wife. So I began to squint as hard as I could to see anything that remotely resembled a Quaker State Motor Oil sign or a Quality Inn sign.

After quite a few signs, I finally saw one that said, "Detroit 37" (miles.) "Detroit," I thought to myself, "that doesn't have a 'Q' in it!" After a few moments it began to dawn on me.

"Wait a second," I said to Debby, "Detroit? Didn't we just past Detroit about an hour and a half ago?"

Without realizing it, my wife and I were so focused on getting the "Q" that we totally lost our perspecitve of where we were and missed our turn going totally around the loop heading back to Detroit!

This incident perfectly parallels how many Christians are living the Christian life. They're focused on the "C's" of children's ministry and choir, the "D's" of discipleship, the "E's" of evangelism, the "F's" of faith—all good things —but they've lost the real reason for doing it.

The ministry that God has given them has become an end in itself, rather than a means to an end . . . an end goal of reaching all ethnic groups for our Lord.

As you read this book and get the Big Picture of what is on God's heart, keep asking yourself the question, "Has my ministry become an end in itself, or is it a means to a greater end that God wants to accomplish through me?"

Bob Sjogren

Bob Sjogren
Co-Founder, FRONTIERS
Associate U.S. Director

Chapter 1

The Story of The Bible

Feel the wind, hot over the scrub out of the foothills on the edge of the desert. Listen to the cracked, dry twitch of locusts. The sun is mercifully fading over this speck of southern Ethiopia. Night is coming quickly, lighting the torches in the boisterous encampment of the semi-nomadic Mursi tribe.

You're sitting in the dirt next to Britisher Malcolm Hunter; you're a link in the great circle surrounding a festive stick-fighting ceremony. You can hardly hear Malcolm over the shouts of the fights, the lowing of the herd surrounding the camp. Nomads are some of the most God-conscious peoples on earth, Malcolm is saying. They live under God's stars, and appoint prayer leaders to pray to the Creator for rain.

Just then an entourage of seven warriors strides before you. They push a huge, muscled old man forward. He's smeared with rancid butter and glistens, stoic as a statue, in the firelight. One who can speak a little Swahili shouts

1

to Malcolm, "He is your brother." Malcolm looks at you. "I must not be understanding him. His Swahili is pretty rough."

"He is your brother," the warrior insists. "He has your blood in him." Through the evening, squinting against the dirt of meandering dust devils in the hot wind and listening over the leaping cracks of the stick-fighting, you piece together bits of the story. The details come later from other participants in one of the striking little dramas God is enacting in every corner of the world.

Saved by the Blood

Decades ago, the Mursi, now about 6,000 strong, were being decimated by a yellow-fever epidemic. The tribe council finally chose eighteen of the strongest warriors to travel to the edge of the bush and find medicine.

After days of walking and near death from the fever, the eighteen staggered into a tiny hut run as a clinic by a young American doctor. The doctor himself had been inoculated against yellow-fever, but he had no yellow-fever antidote. He didn't even have means to take blood-type samples from the dying men. So he did what he could. He inserted a needle into his own arm and began giving blood transfusions to the dying warriors, giving as much blood as he could without losing consciousness.

Fifteen of the men died. Three miraculously survived. In fact, they healed so quickly that within the day they headed back out into the arid bush.

The last of those three legendary warriors stands before you.

Malcolm is excited. He leaps to his feet and begins in pantomime and in trade Swahili to explain to the gathering crowd: "This mighty warrior is a picture to you from the God who sends rain. The God of the stars became a man. He gave his blood to save the Mursi!"

A World-Class Perspective

The significance of this true story? The significance of including you in the scene? Try something: Try imagining God's perspective on what just happened.

The God of the stars, of course, sees the big picture. Look down on the nighttime Mursi celebration with its sudden excitement on hearing the white man's explanation of their tribal legend, of the significance of being saved by blood. Watch the tribesmen scurry over to the elders to pass the word. Notice how many of the people are limping, squinting with eye disease. Pull back and see the cattle herd grazing around the firelit encampment. Notice that the herd, the most valuable possession of the tribe, looks scrawny, sickly.

Glance across time. Catch the significance of God's grand orchestration of events over the years and miles with a mix of factors from yellow-fever infection, to the young Dr. Barlow having no medicine, to a Malcolm Hunter studying nomads and happening upon this small tribe.

Now catch a vision of that grand orchestration. Go

back in time and zoom up from Ethiopia, to squint against the sun retreating across Africa. Peer across the Atlantic northward to the Western Hemisphere, over the full daylight flooding the eastern seaboard of the United States to the flat wheatbelts of North Dakota, where a veterinarian named Gerald is enjoying a lunch of bean soup and homemade bread on a red-checked kitchen table. Between bites he talks with his wife, a nurse, about a tribe he's heard of in Ethiopia. "I think they call 'em the Mursi," he says.

Look west across the Teton mountain range to the morning fog over Washington State. Look down through the mists to see a small morning prayer group crying out to God, wanting to respond to God's heart for the world.

Imagine the joy and sense of purpose that will strike the church members when God answers the longing of their hearts to be significant, to make a difference. Watch through the ensuing months as He leads them to invite a little-known missionary named Malcolm Hunter to speak, as he urges them to adopt a little Ethiopian tribe called the Mursi. Watch the spiritual fireworks when God convinces them to fully underwrite the support of a couple from North Dakota, who are eager to go under the SIM International mission agency. Imagine the spiritual warfare all of these players encounter when the Enemy realizes one of his strongholds is threatened.

Today this drama still goes on. Veterinarian and nurse Gerald and Maija Carlson are, as you read this, living in a shipping crate on the back of a flatbed truck so they can be as mobile as the Mursi. The Washington church, Westminster Chapel of Bellevue, is praying like never before, sending short-term teams to Ethiopia and giving with a vengeance since they're so directly a part of God's big picture. They have made themselves accountable to God for the spiritual welfare of the Mursi.

Malcolm Hunter is pursuing his vision of waking the church to its obligation to the 200 million nomads of the world, who are, almost without exception, peoples without God and without hope.

But what about you? Where are you in this grand scheme?

Perhaps you're feeling restless to be a part of the thousands of daily dramas that make up the big picture of what God is doing in our world. Are you feeling left out of the heart of real, frontline Christianity with its blood, sweat, tears and joy? Are you living a little life in a little world?

It's time to change all that. We'll study some verses, talk through some ideas, think together page after page, and we'll finally finish this book. But be forewarned: The time and effort you put into the book are a drop in the bucket compared to the flood of new insights, experiences and big-picture involvement that will burst into your life after you breeze through this study, after you catch an age-old vision of your part in the history of the world.

Remember the Mursi. Pray for them as a people group to receive the Christ who gave His blood to save them. Pray for the Carlsons and others who are even now being prepared by the God of the universe for their frontline roles in His plan for southern Ethiopia. But pray as well for yourself, that you'll catch a world-class vision of God's heart, of God's perspective during this critical era of our planet. It's no coincidence that you're reading this book now.

The Great Misconception

It's said that the average American evangelical can name about four verses directly related to God's global purpose. A Milwaukee missions committee was recently asked how many they could name, and they came up with two: Matthew 28:19 and Acts 1:8.

But the average evangelical Christian can give four—or let's be kind and say eight. That's eight verses out of 8,000 in the New Testament. Many Christians think, therefore, that God puts about one one-thousandth of a priority on His global purpose, on what we call missions. So giving missions one week out of fifty-two is giving missions a much higher priority than it is due.

An over-emphasis on what God is doing to reach the ends of the earth is even more pronounced if you consider the whole Bible with its 32,000 verses—24,000 in the Old Testament and 8,000 in the New. Eight out of 32,000 verses—that suggests even a lower priority.

Jesus must surely have come to the end of His three-year ministry and at the last moment put his hand to His head as if to say, "Listen, men, I forgot to tell you something!   (Boy, is this embarrassing. I'm about to go to be with the Father . . .) You also need to know that you're supposed to go and reach the nations. I know you've got lots of questions, but I've got to go back to the Father, so I'll send the Holy Spirit to teach you all you're supposed to know about this."   And that was the Great Commission. Somehow we think Jesus gave missions a second-thought emphasis: "Oh, by the way, I forgot to tell you something."

As a result, we Christians sometimes subconsciously think that God gave us missions to inspire the ambitions of zealot misfits. Perhaps God knew He would have some hyperactive Christians who have too much energy to burn, so He planned for them to battle writhing pythons and strike out across the wilds in pith helmets.

This explains how some view the Christian life like a bookshelf. You've got a big book called Discipleship over here, one on music ministry, hefty volumes on marriage and family relationships, and others. Then over there at the end of the shelf is a skinny little brochure. The title—Everything You Always Wanted to Know About Missions.

In reading this book we are going to begin to think differently about the priority of God's global purpose in the Bible. We'll see that the Bible, like any good book, has an introduction, a story and a conclusion. The introduction is found in Genesis 1-11. The story starts in Genesis 12 and runs through to the book of Jude, while the conclusion is found in the book of Revelation. And on a touch-and-go sprint through the Book, we'll perhaps see in a new way how that introduction, storyline, and climax present the big picture of God's heart for the world.

Setting the Scene

Let's look at the Introduction. Scanning through Genesis 1 through 9, we find the bedrock theme of the Bible is redemption: God creates Adam and Eve in a creation that's good, they fall into sin, and God has to sacrifice an animal to show that there must be the shedding of blood for the forgiveness of sins. Then comes the complete corruption of mankind, a penchant for evil that is so grievous that God wipes nearly everyone out with the flood. God shows Noah and his family the rainbow and says, "I'm never going to do that again."

Then comes Genesis 10 and 11. Genesis 10 gives you the Table of the Nations and Genesis 11 begins by explaining what events happened to bring about the Table of Nations. Here, all mankind was of one language and a common speech. It was common for Hebrew writers to write about something very general and then say, "Oh, by the way, let me backtrack and tell you specifically how it happened."

This is the key to understanding the introduction to the story of the Bible. What this simply means is that there was no "us-them" mentality. It wasn't "us" against "them." There was only "us." They were one people with one language and one culture. If their high school team wanted to play somebody in soccer, they had to play intramurals! There was no other "them" to play. But mankind, being evil, wanted to conquer whatever "them" there was. The only "them" was God Himself.

So the people began to build a tower that would reach to heaven. They said, "Come, let us make bricks and bake them thoroughly." They used brick for stone and tar for mortar. "Come, let us build ourselves a city and a tower that reaches to the heavens, so that we may make a name for ourselves and not be scattered over the face of the earth" (Genesis 11:3,4).

They wanted to make a name for themselves. Before whom? Again, before the only Other in existence—before God Himself. Bubbling up among them was tremendous pride as they determined to gain equality with God!

We all know that pride destroys any possible relationship with God. God saw pride welling up to a point where He knew mankind would again—as before the flood—pass the point of ever again turning to Him. Instead of completely destroying the human race, God divided them up by confusing their speech, by separating them into distinct groups of people according to language. It was a divide and conquer strategy. He divided them up so he could "conquer" them later with the Gospel.

If you count the number of groups listed in Genesis

10, you'll find that after the Tower of Babel confusion of languages, there were approximately seventy groups of people on the face of the earth.

So at the end of the introduction to the Story of the Bible, we have the major characters presented: God in heaven and seventy different groups of people on earth.

Now for the Rest of the Story . . .

Endure for a moment a loosely paraphrased Genesis 12:1-3 from the "Sjogren Revised Living Version." It goes like this: God looked down and saw seventy distinct groups of people and He loved every one of them equally. He wanted to reach out to all of them with the blessing of redemption. He could have spoken the gospel to each of them separately, but He chose not to. He chose to use mankind to reach mankind, in order to prepare mankind in the process to rule and reign for eternity.

So, He picked out one of man and said to him, "Abe, I want to bless you. In fact, I want to bless your socks off. I want to pour My grace upon you. I want to give you My Word. I want to give you My Holy Spirit. I want to be your God, and I want you to be My people. The reason that I want to bless you, Abram, is that I love you, but also I want you to turn around and pass My blessings to all those seventy other groups of people that I formed at the Tower of Babel—because I love them too.

"Now Abe, you're not to just sit around in a nice easy chair saying, 'Oh, thank the Lord, I'm blessed.' You're to reach out to those other peoples and tell them what I'm telling you."

The Lord told Abram to leave his country and his people: "Go to a land I will show you. I will make you a great nation and bless you. I will make your name great and you will be a blessing. I will bless those that bless you, and anyone that curses you I will curse. And all peoples of earth will be blessed through you" (Genesis 12:1-3).

Abram (soon to be renamed Abraham) was to be blessed and to be a blessing to every people, tongue, tribe, to every distinct group of people bound by a common culture.

This message was given to Abraham in two very simple parts, in what we'll call the "top line" and the "bottom line." The top line refers to God's blessing of Israel. He wants to bless His people. The bottom line part of the message reveals that He wants His people, not only to enjoy that blessing, but then to turn around and be a blessing to all families on the face of the earth.

Peoples' Power

The terms "families," "peoples," "tongues," "tribes," and "nations" are all synonyms for the same thing: groups of people that call "us" us and "them" them—people bound together by a common language, culture, geography, religion, political system, etc. Back in the time of Babel, people were only bound together linguistically.

Survey your Bible concordance listings of the people-group terms listed above. And remember not to equate peoples with our idea of political countries. For example, the country of India has about 3,000 distinct people groups within its borders. Irian Jaya has about 250 and the Soviet Union more than 500; Pakistan has thirteen. Patrick Johnstone's book *Operation World* can give more specifics relating to this!

The seventy people groups formed at the Tower of Babel split into about 60,000 by the time of Christ, when He commanded us to make disciples of every nation or, literally, people group. Today there are about 24,000 distinct people groups—a smaller number due to communications, technology, air travel, etc.

Who are the unreached people groups of our planet?

The 1,500 nomadic Chang-pa of northern India, the 20 million Sundanese of Indonesia, the Engenni of Nigeria, the Wenki of China, the Gilyak of Russia, the Fulnio of Brazil. . . and about 11,994 more!

Twelve thousand people groups are currently being discipled. The other 12,000, mostly among the Muslim, Chinese, Hindu, Buddhist and tribal cultures, have no church among them and little or no mission work.

Look at that bottom line in Genesis 12:3 for one very simple little word. God said "all." All of the peoples of the earth are to be blessed. That's a very significant word. God wanted to reach every distinct group of people on the face of the earth. This means what we actually have here in Genesis 12:1-3 is the Great Commission!

Most believers think Jesus first gave the Great Commission. Actually, Jesus reviewed the Great Commission. The Great Commission was given right here in Genesis 12. Abraham was commissioned to reach all the nations on the face of the earth, to "go therefore, and make disciples of all nations."

The Great Commission is the foundation for the Story of the Bible. This commissioning begins a song that's sung from the very beginning to the very end of the story, a song we have in some of our modern hymnals: "Let every kindred, every tribe on this terrestrial ball, to Him all majesty ascribe and crown Him Lord of all. . ."

This story keeps going on. . . . .

God's destination for Israel was a land flowing with milk and honey. Does the Promised Land suggest the top line or the bottom line of blessing? The top line, of course. But with every top line blessing comes a bottom line responsibility. What is the bottom line responsibility linked to the blessing of such a land?

The Promised Land was a very strategic piece of property. It was located in the center of the nations on the face of the earth: "Thus saith the Lord God, This is Jerusalem. I have set it in the midst of the nations and countries round about her" (Ezekiel 5:5). Scholars say that most of the major trading routes of the world passed right through Jerusalem.

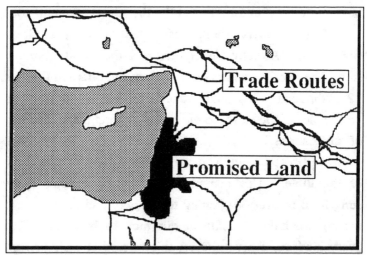

Imagine: While the merchants were trading, they would talk with the Jews, asking them about their God: "Show me your God. It's going to be a rough trip home, and

I need extra luck. So I'm offering sacrifices to as many gods as I can. Where's your God?"

And the Jews would answer, "I'm sorry, we don't have an idol that we worship. Our God is the God of the heavens and the earth."

They would reply: "You're kidding! You don't have an idol? Every other nation does."

"We don't."

"Well, what's this God's name?" And the Jews would begin to go over the names of God: Jehovah-Jireh, "God is our provider."

"You mean your God provides for you?" the traders would ask.

"Yes, let me tell you how it happened." And they'd begin to testify about how God provided.

"What?, your God is 'The Lord-Your-Righteousness'?"

"Yes," the Jews would answer, "He is our righteousness."

"Tell me about it. How do you have righteousness through your God?" On and on went the questions.

As the caravans wound out of the Promised Land toward the east or south or north, this network of merchants would keep talking about the nation that doesn't have a god they can see; the God of the Jews, they'd say, claims to be the God above all gods. We'll find later in our study that as this news began to spread, God's reputation went to the very ends of the earth.

Song of the Nations

Later in Israel's history, King David sings a prayer:

Give thanks to the Lord, call on his name;
Make known among the nations what he has done.
Declare his glory among the nations,
His marvelous deeds among all peoples. . .
Ascribe to the Lord, O families of nations;
Ascribe to the Lord glory and strength. . .
Let the heavens rejoice, let the earth be glad.
Let them say among the nations, 'The Lord reigns!'
(1 Chronicles 16:8,23,28,31).

Here it is again—the Great Commission, not in its original form but a lyrical rendering of the Jews' bottom line responsibility. It's a Davidic version of the good old gospel song "We've a Story to Tell to the Nations!"

Keep in mind that the Israelites did sing these song—psalms—regularly as one of the key methods of preserving the stories of their heritage from generation to generation. Poets and singers weren't incidental entertainers in most ancient cultures; they were revered as the historians, the keepers of tradition. For example, notice God's command to Moses to write down this song "and teach it to the Israelites and have them sing it so that it may be a witness for me." (Deuteronomy 31:19).

Let's go quickly on to Psalm 87 and see the story unfold even more. Most of us know there is going to be a book in heaven called the Book of Life. But did you know there is a whole library in heaven—not just a book? In Daniel 7:10 we have "books" being opened, in Daniel 10:21 we have the Book of Truth, in Malachi 3:16 we have the Book of Remembrances, and here we find another book.

The Register of the Peoples

Begin looking at verse 4 in Psalm 87: "I will record Rahab [Egypt] and Babylon among those who acknowledge me."

Regardless of how we or early Israel viewed those groups, God states that the Egyptians and Babylonians are among those who acknowledged Him.

"Philistia, too; Tyre, along with Cush [Ethiopia], will say, This one and that one were born in Zion."

Think it through: Were these Egyptians and Babylonians actually, physically born in Zion? Did they adhere to the dietary code, the customs of that time for the Jewish people?

If so, they would have been called "Jews." But they're not. They're called Babylonians, Egyptians, Ethiopians. And they've been born into a spiritual Zion. If we can borrow new Testament terminology, they've been born into the Kingdom of God or the "church." Now for a surprising insight into God's heart for every people group of the world: "The Lord will write in the register of the peoples, this one was born in Zion."

The Register of the Peoples! God has a book in heaven,

and He's keeping track of every distinct ethnic group that has ever existed on the face of the earth.

Why would God register every distinct ethnic group that has ever existed? Because He made a promise to Abraham to reach every one of them, and He's going to be faithful in tracking that promise. Is He doing it to jog His own memory, scratching His head, asking: "Hey, Abe. Did I reach those Kurds in Iraq yet? I'm not sure, could you check the register please?" No, He's doing it to provide a witness and testimony to His faithfulness: Showing that for all of eternity, He was faithful in offering the blessing of salvation to every people, tribe and nation.

There are many references to God's global purpose in the Old Testament. We will catch more later, but for our initial overview, let's scan a couple of key New Testament passages. Does Jesus deal with the Abrahamic Covenant's bottom line resonsibility to be a blessing to every people? Or did He come to His disciples and say, "Look, you want to know why it's called the Old Testament, it's because it's old. . . outdated. Let me give you some fresh material and we can call it the New Testament!"

The Upper-Room Seminar

Let's look quickly at Luke 24:45-47.

Jesus has lived His life on the earth, has died, and has been resurrected from the dead after three days. Notice that He's not telling the disciples, "I'm alive again! Death has no hold on me. Let's praise the Lord together!"

Instead, He's giving His disciples a forty-day crash course in reviewing the Great Commission, in which He held the "Upper-Room-Seminar." And that's where we find Him in Luke 24:45. . .

"Then He opened their minds so they could understand the Scriptures." Catch the significance of this. Jesus is about to open up all of Scripture and explain it to His disciples.

How many themes do you think Jesus would have to address in order to do justice to all of the Scriptures? If I were to quiz you to name a major theme that Jesus would have to address, what would you say? Grace? Mercy? Love? And how many major themes would He cover? Ten? Thirty?

Interestingly, Jesus breaks all of the Scriptures down into two central themes. Let's look at them.

Jesus says, "This is what is written: The Christ will suffer and rise from the dead on the third day." That's the first theme: suffering, rising from the dead on the third day. He's speaking of the forgiveness of sins, about a relationship we can have with our God. And then He explains "that repentance and forgiveness of sins will be preached in His name to all nations, beginning at Jerusalem. You are witnesses of these things." The second theme is that His Name should go to all the nations on the face of the earth.

Sounds a bit familiar, doesn't it?

That He should suffer and rise from the dead on

the third day to provide salvation seems to refer to what part of the covenant? Top line. And "that repentance and forgiveness of sins should be preached in His name to all nations" refers, of course, to the bottom line of the covenant. Jesus broke all the Scriptures down into two central themes: top line and bottom line.

Now is this really true? Can you buy that? Let's put it to the test. There was an expert of the law who came up to test Jesus. He asked Him, "Which is the greatest of all the commands?" What did Jesus say? "Love the Lord your God with all your heart, soul, mind and strength" which refers to what part of the covenant? Top line. And, even though the questioner didn't ask for it, Jesus went on to say that the second is like the first: "You shall love your neighbor as yourself." This sounds vaguely related to the bottom line. But His answer doesn't have a specifically cross-cultural emphasis.

So, when the seeker said, "But, Jesus, who is my neighbor?" what did Jesus bring in? The example of one from another people group, a Samaritan, a cross-cultural emphasis. Jesus broke the Scriptures into two themes: top line and bottom line.

Look also at the ten commandments. The first four deal with your relationship to God, which deals with what part of the covenant? Right, the top! The next six deal with your relationship to man. . . the bottom line of the covenant.

Is this new to you? No, not at all. You've just heard

it in other phrases such as "to know Him and make Him known" or "your vertical relationship to God and your horizontal relationship to others." But now there's clarification. It is to make Him known to all nations; a horizontal relationship cross-culturally. It has been there the whole time.

Obviously, if I'm focusing on the top line of the covenant only and saying, "I repent and receive the blessings of salvation, so God bless me, God bless us, God bless my family, God bless our church, God bless my community," I've missed half of Christianity. The other half of Christianity is turning around with that blessing and reaching out cross-culturally to the world.

Now, imagine that God had said to Abraham, "Look, I want to bless you so that you can be a blessing. Period." What would that mean? It would mean that all Abraham would have to do is reach out to people in his own culture, his own community, his own ethnic group, and God would be pleased. But God did not say "share this blessing with your family, your neighbors, with people who are like you." He said, "Through you all peoples on earth shall be blessed."

God wanted Abraham to be involved in some type of cross-cultural ministry. And, emphasized here again in the New Testament, He wants the same for us. He blessed us to be involved in reaching the nations. We'll hit the implications of that mandate later, since most believers feel a little uncomfortable about it. But let's plant it firmly somewhere in your gray matter: We believers are to have a cross-cultural impact in reaching all the nations to fulfill the promise God made to Abraham some 4,000 years ago.

We'll look more carefully through the New Testament later for this top line—bottom line theme. But for now, notice: When Jesus opened up the disciples' minds to understand the Scriptures, did He open their eyes to the New Testament only? to the New and Old Testament together? or just to the Old Testament? Of course it was just to the Old, because the New Testament had not been written yet.

Where do you think Jesus turned to in the Old Testament to prove that repentance and forgiveness of sins should be preached to "all nations"?

Well, the text doesn't tell us, but we can make a

pretty good educated guess that it was Genesis 12:3. How? Because now all of the disciples begin to quote Genesis l2:3—the original source Jesus must have highlighted in the Old Testament scrolls.

Peter, standing before the Sanhedrin in Acts 3:25-26, quotes from the second half of verse 3 in Genesis 12. He didn't quote the first part of the verse, because he knew they knew that God wanted to bless them. But he knew they were unaware that God wanted them to turn around and be a blessing cross-culturally. Paul, writing to the Galatians, a Gentile people, also quotes Genesis l2:3 (Galatians 3:8). The writer to the Hebrews quotes Genesis l2:3 (Hebrews 6:13-17).

What are they doing? They're quoting the original source that Jesus gave in that "Upper-Room Seminar." He took out a pink flourescent highlighter and went over the verse again and again! That's why they remember it and quote it first.

Do you see that Jesus never "gave" the Great Commission? He reviewed the Great Commission of Genesis 12, and the disciples quoted that original mandate in their writings. Because Jesus turned to the Old Testament Scriptures to prove that the Gospel was to go out to all nations, missions had to be firmly embedded in the Old Testament. . . . That's why it forms the story of the Bible.

In Galilee and Jerusalem and Judea . . . ?
Let's look at a final passage in our sprint through

the Story of the Bible. In Acts 2, we find Jesus already ascended into heaven. We find the disciples obeying Jesus' words: "You shall receive power when the Holy Spirit comes on you; and you will be my witnesses in Jerusalem, and in all Judea and Samaria, and to the ends of the earth" (Acts 1:8).

Jesus told the disciples to go back to Jerusalem. Why? Many evangelical Christians say, "Oh, I know what that means. If we're to go back to Jerusalem, we're supposed to go back to our own community. The disciples were going back to their own areas, their own towns. We're supposed to start in Jerusalem, our hometown. That's where we start sharing our faith."

Wrong . . . . I'm sorry, but the disciples were not from Jerusalem.

Read with me in Acts 2:6: "When they heard this sound, a crowd came together in bewilderment, because each one heard them speaking in his own language. Utterly amazed, they asked: 'Are not all these men who are speaking Galileans?'"

Now, how did they know the disciples were Galileans? Because the disciples all had strange accents; they didn't speak like the people in Jerusalem. They were in foreign territory.

Why had Jesus told them to go to a place which was not their home? Verse 5 has the key. "Now there were staying in Jerusalem God-fearing Jews from every nation under heaven." Our God is a strategic God. He gave the Jews the Promised Land so they could teach all the nations by being in the center.

He said to go to Jerusalem because He knew in Jerusalem there were God-fearing Jews from every nation on the face of the earth, and He knew that would be the impetus to start a worldwide movement that would spread to the very ends of the earth.

Why did God have the disciples speak in Gentile languages? This was to emphasize that the Holy Spirit was not given to them merely for their own enrichment, pleasure, and edification, but to show that the Gospel was for all people—to the very ends of the earth.

It was a missionary move, strategically planned by God, so that all nations would have a chance to hear the Gospel. God planted the disciples not in their hometowns but in the most strategic place to further His ironclad promise to bless all nations.

The Story of the Bible. It starts in Genesis, runs through the Old Testament and flows into the New. It's a cohesive theme, unifying all sixty-six books of the Bible to form one story—God's desire to see every nation reached through the message of redemption. It's there.

The Conclusion

But how does the Story of the Bible end? Well, don't tell anyone, but let's cheat and peek in the back of the book!

In Revelation 5:9 we find a song that's being sung

by the Elders and the living creatures. If the Elders and the living creatures are singing this song, it must be very important. Such a key song will probably be sung over and over and over again. So if you haven't memorized the song yet, you'd better memorize it before you go to be with the Lord. Wouldn't you be embarrassed to have to say, "Excuse me, I never learned this song. Are there any handouts, please . . .?"

Listen to the song. Imagine the melody. Try to picture the setting: The elders and the living creatures are gathered around the throne singing, "You are worthy to take the scroll and to open its seals, because you were slain, and with your blood you purchased men for God from just about every tongue, tribe, people and nation."

Obviously, that is not what the Word of God says. It actually says, "You are worthy because with your blood you purchased men for God from every tongue, tribe, people and nation. You have made them to be a kingdom of priests to serve our God, and they will reign on the earth" (Revelation 5:9).

The plan God laid out in Genesis 12—to reach every distinct ethnic group on the face of the earth with His offer of redemption—is finished. The Story ends.

But perhaps there is a doubting Thomas up in heaven who starts yelling, "Stop the music, stop the singing, hold everything. How do we know this Lamb has redeemed people from every tongue and tribe and nation? How do we know He's worthy?"

What's Abraham going to do? Is he going to walk hastily over to Thomas and say, "Look, Tom, you blew it down there on earth, don't blow it up here in heaven. Just keep quiet?" He's more likely to put his arm around Thomas and say, "Look, Tom, go down through the clouds twenty kilometers and take a left." (Okay, guys, it's going to be kilometers in heaven, not miles, let's get used to it.) "Then you'll hit a thunderstorm. Take a right at the thunderstorm and there you will find a library. Walk in past three aisles and on the left you'll find a book called The Register of the Peoples. Look under the listing of every distinct ethnic group that ever existed on the face of the earth and see if you do not find at least a few individuals who are represented here from every group.

"You can check, Thomas, but I guarantee you—He's been found worthy." The Register of the Peoples is a written testimony of what He has done.

Study Break

Worn out after our run through the Bible? Provoked by more questions than answers? Great! Then you're primed for a bit more intensive study of the big picture of God's purpose and your part in it.

But before you rush into our next chapter, think through "For Further Thought" on the next page.

And be accountable: Pray for the events God is now directing among one of the planet's people groups yet to be discipled. Pray for God's blessing on the Mursi of Ethiopia, who already are familiar with what it means to be saved by the blood.

For Further Thought

To reinforce the concept of topline and bottomline blessings, write out an explanation of this idea as if to a child.

Count your blessings! Then, in each category, list a possible bottom line responsibility that matches each blessing.

Top line Blessings — Bottom line Responsibilities
Spiritual:
Physical:
Relational:
Financial:
List other ideas new to you from this chapter's discussion.
List questions raised in this segment of study.
Scan the chapter, noting especially meaningful references. Mark these in your personal study Bible.
Memorize Revelation 5:9 and pray for those Ethiopian Mursi people who will be there!

Chapter 2

God Swears . . .

You're moving west around the globe, into the country of Mali in your trek across the sub-Sahara of Africa. With the Ethiopian Mursi people fresh in your mind, you meet up with a maverick named Randy. . . .

Red, powder-soft dust puffs in your window and up through the floorboards of the Land Rover. You're riding shotgun as Djibi drives and intently tells you a long story in a French dialect you don't understand. He watches your reactions for minutes at a time, smiling through the dust as you nervously worry about his staying on the track that wanders haphazardly through the West African 130-degree afternoon.

Lean Randy Cresswell, hiking-booted and sweating profusely, bounces in the open back of the Rover along with four more of his Muslim convert disciples he calls the "A-Team."

He has told you about last night's disastrous attempt to show the Jesus evangelistic film in a tiny Mali village.

Five minutes into the film, a wild windstorm leaped out of the desert to slap over the screen and knock the projector into the dirt. Now you're all heading to the village of Karaya. A Christian family hosting one of the region's first Christian weddings is planning to witness to their hundreds of Muslim relatives and wedding guests by showing the film. But the projector is permanently damaged; Randy and the A-Team had stayed up most of the night trying to repair it. Jesus will be a no-show at the wedding, and you can tell Randy is feeling the discouragement of it all.

You recall the passage of Randy's newsletter you'd read on the plane from Addis to Bamako: "The unremitting heat is balanced by incessant dust. Much more discomforting than this was a series of organizational decisions that were tearing me up inside. We just came out last week from under another financial crisis. The daily round of problem-solving seems to be grinding what remains of my vigor and vitality. . . ."

Glance at Randy now in the back. He smiles back at you and tips his hat. You turn back to squint through the dirt-packed windshield and wonder what drives a man to live on the edge of the world like this.

Cursed Traitors To Allah

Djibi pulls up under parched shade trees at the crumbly bank of the surging, half-mile-wide Senegal River. Randy climbs out, stretches and says, "Must've opened a gate up at the dam. Can't drive it. Guess we'll have to swim."

Your voice creaks with dust: "Swim?"

He smiles, swings a blue nylon backpack over his shoulder and scrambles down the bank. The A-Team graciously gestures for you to follow.

After the half mile of shoulder-deep wading, you emerge on the opposite bank in questionable shape for a wedding. The warm river water evaporates from your skin so quickly that you feel suddenly chilled.

Two young Kassonke boys from Kayaya run to meet you. "No Jesus film," Randy apologizes, and they run back to the village a quarter mile away with the embarrassing, disappointing news.

In the village, so much preparation is bustling around you that you're hardly noticed. That afternoon you trek with Randy and Djibi four sweltering miles to the young man's village. When you arrive, Djibi's foster father stands in his doorway and refuses to allow any of you Christians— Djibi included—into his house. The man curses you as traitors to Allah.

You trudge back to Karaya to find a distinguished girot, a professional dance master, choreographing the antics of his dance troupe in traditional wedding dances. The parents of the groom dramatically apologize to each arriving guest, with a nod toward you and Randy, that there'll be no film as promised. There'll only be the dances. The usual.

"You okay?" you ask Randy, as you both, totally exhausted,

lean against a rough stone corral to watch the dances.

He's authentic. "At the end of my energy, ideas and emotions, frankly," he says.

It's fully dark now and the temperature cools to 110 degrees. Randy leans over to you with a glint in his eye. "Ask Toumani for me if he thinks I could portray the crucifixion in a dance."

Toumani, one of the A-Team, says, "No."

Randy nods in the firelight and tells you, "I always follow my guys' advice. Almost always." But the glint in his eye remains. Suddenly, during a lull in the professional troupe's repertoire, Randy leaps into the center of the festivities—hiking boots, shirt sweat-soaked, a crazy foreigner with a stick as his only prop.

The Messiah Dance

Something happens. The Kassonke crowds stop milling around the dance area. The faces are awe-struck as they watch this white man leap about, plod with a cross on his back, spin, hang on a crossbeam, die and bury himself in the dirt. The air is electric, intense. The one dancer stirs, leaps into the air, alive again in resurrection. Dozens of Muslim men rush over to the A-Team with questions about the meaning of the dance.

After ten minutes of improvisation in a totally unfamiliar art form, Randy stops, beyond exhaustion. He, too, is besieged with questions. You understand some of the French: "What was the death for? He lives after the death? What does this mean?"

Randy staggers over to you and shrugs foolishly. He's painted in sweaty dust. The head girot rushes over and insists that Randy teach him this "Messiah Dance" and explain exactly what it means. The night crackles with the issue of the risen Christ as the disciples continue to field a deluge of questions.

After a half-hour's practice, the girot and Randy step together into the dance ring and, in precise movements, dance the story again. Afterward, around every torch, the entire village is buzzing with the story and the A-Team's explanations. By now it's about one o'clock in the morning. Randy motions for you to head with him down to the river to wash some of the burial dirt off. He can hardly walk.

Stumbling in the black darkness near the river, you suddenly stop and listen. The voice of the head girot grandly announces that everyone is to listen to the complete story of the Messiah Dance. And you foreigners stand dumbfounded as the girot's voice rings out explaining the life, the death, the resurrection of Jesus Christ. Some of the phrases he's borrowed from Randy's explanation, some from stories he's probably heard previously. But some of the truths this Muslim dance master preaches to the spellbound crowd are so biblically accurate and convicting that Randy shrugs and says, "Well, God spoke through a donkey, didn't He?"

The miraculous evening is only an initial breakthrough;

no Muslims convert on the spot. But days later, as you head for the airport to fly out of Bamako to Casablanca, and eventually New York, you hear that the Messiah Dance is being performed at wedding after wedding among the Kassonke people. The Muslim girots at each dance troupe's "Messiah" performance, of course, must explain this new cultural fad's significance. Muslim dancers are proclaiming the Gospel!

At the airport, you glance at the note Randy handed you: "Paul says, 'The important thing is that in every way . . . Christ is preached. And because of this I rejoice' (Philippians 1:18). I firmly believe that God arranged the people and personalities, the weather patterns and whatever else to bring that evening to pass, and I'm confident that He who has begun this good work—as strange as it is—will perform it until the day of Christ!"

You board the old prop plane to leave the dust and heat of mid-Africa behind—the daily fare for Randy and other missionaries, who are dead-set on reaching these unreached people with the blessing of redemption. You vow never to forget the crazy, striking scene of the first "Messiah Dance." You pray now for the Kassonke to embrace that Messiah. Scratching your head, you are amazed at how committed God must be to this small tribe somewhere in the middle of nowhere.

The Commitment
God's promise to reach all the nations through Abraham

was repeated four more times after its initial declaration in Genesis 12:1-3. Twice more to Abraham himself, once to Isaac, and once to Jacob. But He did something very peculiar in that third reinforcement.

God repeats the promise a third time in Genesis 22:15: "The angel of the Lord called to Abraham from heaven a second time and said, 'I swear by myself, declares the Lord, because you have done this and have not withheld your son, your only son, I will surely bless you and make your descendants as numerous as the stars of the sky and as the sands of the seashore. Your descendants will take possession of the cities of their enemies and through your offspring all nations on earth shall be blessed."

Read back through that rendition of the covenant to notice the top line and bottom line of the blessing. Then think through that peculiar clause, "I swear by myself."

In Abraham's day, swearing was the equivalent of signing your name on the dotted line. Today we sign our name; back then they swore by something greater than themselves. They'd swear by God, or by heaven, or by the altar. But when God wants to impress on Abraham that He is signing on the dotted line, how can He swear by something greater than Himself?

The only thing that He could do to assure Abraham of the seriousness of this promise was to swear by His own Name. He said, "I swear by Myself." Forgive another loose paraphrase, but it's as if God said, "If there's anything you can bet your bottom dollar on, it's that I'll bless you,

Abraham, and that you'll be a blessing to all the nations of the earth. This is one thing you can count on: It will happen!"

God comes to Isaac in Genesis 25:3-4, saying, "What I told your father, the same thing holds true for you. I'll bless you to be a blessing to all the nations on the face of the earth." He comes to Jacob: "Jacob, I spoke to your father, I spoke to your grandfather as well, and the same thing holds true for you. I'll bless you so that you can be a blessing to all the families on the face of the earth" (Genesis 28:14).

God expresses this covenant five times in this opening development of the Story of the Bible. He uses this repetition to focus attention on the promise itself—repeating to make it a high priority at the very beginning of His Word.

He must have done this because He knows how many people can major on the minors and minor on the majors. So He tells us at the beginning of the Bible that this is extremely significant information; this is what we need to major on . . . reaching all the nations on the face of the earth with His blessing of redemption.

Let's quickly glance forward through Scripture and see how this top line—bottom line story unfolds.

God's Bottom Line Strategies

Notice, for instance, the creative imagery God used to remind the fledgling Hebrew nation of His covenant with Abraham, Isaac and Jacob. As the children of Israel journeyed into the wilderness, they came to Elim, "where there were twelve springs and seventy palm trees and they camped there near the waters" (Exodus 15:27).

An oasis with twelve springs giving life to seventy palm trees.

Do those numbers sound familiar? Twelve springs could easily represent the twelve tribes of Israel. Seventy palm trees could easily represent the seventy nations on the face of the earth of Genesis 11. And the object lesson is obvious: The twelve tribes of Israel were God's provision to give life to all the nations now scattered to the ends of the earth.

Blessed to Be a Blessing

Speaking of lyrical renditions of the Great Commission, let's follow The Story of the Bible into the Psalms. In Psalm 67 we find again the basic structure of the covenant given to Abraham. The New American Standard Bible gives a specific translation here: "God be gracious to us and bless us and cause His face to shine upon us. Selah." You've probably heard that first part of verse 1 many times. Is it top line or bottom line theology? Top line— which may be why it is so familiar. Then, as we're learning to expect, comes the bottom line: "That Thy way may be known on the earth, Thy salvation among all nations."

Read through the rest of the Psalm:

Let the peoples praise Thee, O God;
Let all the peoples praise Thee.

Let the nations be glad and sing for joy;
For Thou wilt judge the peoples with uprightness,
And guide the nations on the earth.
Let the peoples praise Thee, O God;
Let all the peoples praise Thee.
The earth has yielded its produce;
God, our God, blesses us. . . .

That all the ends of the earth may fear Him.

Notice carefully the final verse: "God blesses us, that
. . ." Why does God bless us? "That all the ends of
the earth may fear Him."

God blesses us to be a blessing to the ends of the
earth. If we try to hoard His blessing for ourselves, we're
missing half of what God wants for us—to be a blessing
cross-culturally. With every top line blessing comes a
bottom line responsibility.

The Great Feast

In Isaiah 25:6-7, we catch a glimpse of who is going
to be listed in that registry of the peoples. Visualize
the future with Isaiah: "On this mountain, the Lord the
Almighty will prepare a feast of rich food for all people,
a banquet of aged wine, the best of meats and the finest
of wines. On this mountain He will destroy the shroud
that enfolds all peoples, the sheet that covers all nations;
He will swallow up death forever. The Sovereign Lord
will wipe away the tears from all faces. He will remove
the disgrace of His people from all the earth. The Lord

has spoken."

There's going to be a feast in heaven where God takes away the blindness of the nations and brings representatives from each of them into His kingdom.

Crashing the Party?

Let's think together through Matthew 8:5-12, the classic story of the faith of a Roman centurion.   Keep in mind the context: The Jews have been overrun by the Romans. The centurion in this passage was a Gentile, whom the Jews commonly referred to as "dogs." God's chosen people knew that God blesses the Jewish people, but not those Gentile dogs.

When Jesus had entered Capernaum, a centurion came to him, asking for help.   "Lord," he said, "my servant lies at home paralyzed and in terrible suffering." Jesus said to him, "I will go and heal him."

Now, for Jesus to say that He would go to the house of a Gentile was very much against the cultural norm (even though some of the elders were encouraging him to do this).   But Jesus showed parity (beyond the elder's encouragement) for the Gentiles, so Gentiles could have a part of God's blessing. "The centurion replied, 'Lord, I do not deserve to have you come under my roof. But just say the word, and my servant will be healed....'"

When Jesus heard this, He was astonished and said to those elders following him, "Humph, not bad for a Gentile." Is that what He said?

No.

Jesus turned to these elders and said, "I have not found anyone in Israel with such great faith." He's talking about a Gentile who has great faith. He didn't exactly say this to get on the good side of the elders, you realize. He said it to inflict a wound. And then after inflicting the wound, He began to rub salt in it to make sure it hurt.

Notice verse 11 of Matthew 8: "For I say to you that many will come from the east and the west, and will take their places at the feast with Abraham, Isaac and Jacob in the kingdom of heaven. But the subjects of the kingdom will be thrown outside, into the darkness, where there will be weeping and gnashing of teeth."

Now perhaps you've read these verses and thought, "Lord, this sequence does not make sense. We were talking about the great faith of this centurion and then suddenly you're talking about some meal up in heaven—something entirely different! Why?" Let's analyze the sequence.

The passage says that many will come from the east and the west, and Luke adds the "north and south." (Thanks, Luke.) North and south and east and west of where? Well, where they were—the Promised Land. What's north and south and east and west of the Promised Land? The nations, peoples, Gentiles—which is another way of saying "all nations on the face of the earth."

Jesus is saying there will be representatives from every distinct ethnic group taking their places at the feast with

Abraham, Isaac and Jacob. We're reminded of the passage in Isaiah 25 we looked at briefly; there'll be a multi-ethnic feast in heaven!

Now, a feast is a time to celebrate. In many Middle Eastern cultures, a good feast lasts sometimes up to a week. You can have a feast to celebrate a wedding, a birth, a religious holiday. (Today's "feasts" would occur any time you have a good excuse to have a party!) There's going to be a celebration in heaven with Gentiles from all over, and at the head of the table are Abraham, Isaac and Jacob. But why them?

Did you ever wonder why God refers to Himself as the God of Abraham, Isaac and Jacob? Ever study their lives? Abraham's life was pretty good. As the father of our faith, there were a few times when he flagrantly lied to try to save himself. But let's rate him 70% good, 30% bad—we'll give him that much credit.

How about Isaac's life? He didn't do anything great; he didn't do anything that bad. There's a hint in the Scripture that he could have conquered some people through war, but he chose not to. Sort of a boring list of accomplishments for a patriarch, wouldn't you say?

Then we look at Jacob's life—Jacob "the mischievous one, the deceiver." Jacob's sons lie to him his entire life about his favorite son Joseph. He and his family face famine, and they go to the Gentile dogs of Egypt to beg for food. Now, why would God call Himself the God of Jacob?

Why not the God of Moses? The events he did for Moses were very impressive in the eyes of the world. Fifteen hundred years later the nations still remembered the Red Sea story.

But God calls Himself the God of Abraham, the God of Isaac and the God of Jacob because Abraham, Isaac and Jacob were the three men to whom He made a commitment to reach all the people groups on the earth. When God refers to Himself as the God of Abraham, Isaac and Jacob, it's as if He's saying, "You want to know my calling card? You want to know what I want to be known by? I'm the God who spoke to these three men to redeem and to bless every distinct ethnic group on the face of the earth. That's what I want to be known for."

So let's go back to the text in Matthew 8. There will be Gentiles from the north, south, east and west coming to a feast to celebrate something, and at the head of the table will be Abraham, Isaac and Jacob. What will they be celebrating?

The fulfillment of the promise that God gave to those three men to reach every ethnic group on the face of the earth. They'll be celebrating forever and ever. And you and I will be there.

Notice the text says the representatives of these people groups will "take their places," not "crash the party." They will take their places at the feast with Abraham, Isaac and Jacob—places reserved for them.

The Great Re-Commission

I think we've caught the idea now that Jesus did not give the Great commission in Matthew 28:18-20; He simply reviewed it. But let's look at the "Great Commission" one last time to see if we can find something new.

"All authority in heaven and on earth has been given to me. Therefore go and make disciples of all nations, baptizing them in the name of the Father and of the Son and of the Holy Spirit, and teaching them to obey everything I have commanded you. And surely I will be with you always, to the very end of the age."

Unfortunately, our English language doesn't do justice to these verses. There are four verbs in this passage. The main action verb is not "go," but "make disciples." This is the main emphasis that Jesus was giving.

In Greek as well as in English, there are verb transitives and verb intransitives. A verb transitive is a type of verb that has to transfer meaning to an object. If I were to say the word "throw," you would say, "Throw what? What do I throw?" There has to be something after the word "throw," in order for it to make sense.

This is the same with "make disciples." This isn't a mandate to make disciples as was ordered in 2 Timothy 2:2. If someone opens up to Matthew 28:20 and encourages you from that passage to disciple men and women, they are misusing the Scriptures. We are to do this, but you don't get that idea here.

What follows "make disciples" is "all nations." How

do you disciple a nation? Do you pull a nation into your living room and hold a Bible study? Of course not. So how do you do it?

Jesus gave us the answer in the latter part of the verse: "baptizing them . and . teaching . them." Baptizing gets individuals to identify with Christ, to stand up and say, "Yes, I am one of His disciples. I identify with Him." Teaching them to obey the Scriptures is the second part.

What do we have when we have a group of individuals identifying with Christ and being obedient to the Scriptures? A church. What Jesus was really saying was, "Go to every distinct ethnic group on the face of the earth and start a church." We have an equal-opportunity God. He wants every group of people to have an equal opportunity to say "yes" or "no" to Him.

Think about it: Perhaps the reason many believers are reluctant to see their lives focused on God's great purpose as revealed in the Great Commission is because they know making a disciple of every person will never happen. After all, Christ Himself states that "the gate is small, and the way is narrow that leads to life, and few are those who find it" (Matthew 7:14).

If we secretly think the Great Commission is unrealistic, that it only expresses Jesus' desire to see "all creatures" become disciples, then of course it won't be a realistic part of our lives.

But mark it down for now: We're to make disciples of all 'ethne,' of all people groups. And you just might get excited as later in our study we see how realistic that mandate is, how many ethnic groups have been "made disciples," how many ethnic groups haven't, how much more we have to do to actually, finally fulfill the Great Commission that God gave us back in Genesis 12.

Yes, I'm talking about us—you and me living within sight of reaching every people group on the globe.

Let's look at one final passage in the conclusion to the Story: "And this gospel of the kingdom will be preached in all the world as a testimony to all nations, and then the end will come (Mt. 24:14)."

And then the end will come. What is the end? Fortunately, this isn't a study on the eschatological ramifications of the ineffable multi-millennial. There are plenty of volumes that wrangle about the timing of that particular phrase.

But the essence of the statement is clear: There is a direct link in the Bible between the end coming and God reaching all the nations on the face of the earth. Why is God concerned about reaching all the peoples on the face of the earth before the end? Because He made a promise to Abraham. And if God does not fulfill that promise, what can God be called for all of eternity? A liar. Can you imagine believers in heaven saying, "Not bad. All the groups but thirteen are represented. Hey, who's counting? God almost fulfilled His word."

God cannot be called a liar for all of eternity—it is impossible. Write it down as a solid fact: All nations will be reached, and then the end will come.

His Greatest Glory

But how does all of this fit into glorifying God? Isn't that supposed to be the central purpose of man? Think of this.

Have you ever seen internationals come to know the Lord? It's pretty exciting, isn't it, to bow in unified prayer with a person from a totally different perspective and culture! What does that do to your vision of God? It expands it, causes it to grow, to explode!

There's a principle in that. God gets greater glory by bringing unity out of that which is diverse. When a Jordanian Muslim-Convert and an Jewish-Believer unite in Jesus' name, the world stands in awe of the power of the Gospel.

How then could we give God the maximum amount of glory He could ever have? Of course, by bringing representatives from every tongue, tribe and nation to the knowledge of God's goodness and grace. That's the true motivation for missions. To work toward the goal of bringing God the maximum amount of glory for all of eternity.

For Further Thought

For individual or group study.

What difference does a top line-bottom line perspective make on our understanding of Scripture? Complete the sentences below from a top line—bottom line perspective:

God calls Himself the God of Abraham, Issac and Jacob

because...

Jesus never really gave the Great Commission because....

The basic unifying theme of all Scripture is...

Although other passages command me to be a witness to everyone around me on the home front, Acts 1:8 isn't a verse on reaching my own neighborhood because...

List ideas new to you from this chapter's discussion.

List questions raised in this segment of study.

Scan the last two chapters, noting especially meaningful references. Mark these down in your personal Bible and pray for Randy and the Kossanke people.

Chapter 3

Self Centered Evangelical Christianity

You've flown in from London, back to the USA, and you can't wait to get to the washing machine to get the Sahara dust out of your clothes. As you load in the detergent, you're wondering more than ever how God's people in America fit into the closing stages of God's purpose to bless every people group on earth. You know the history of the amazing Student Volunteer Movement and the resulting surge in mission activity bursting from this continent a hundred years ago.

You're aware of the wave of new missionaries who, following World War II, left houses and lands to make Christ known among the nations—such as the moderate response to General Douglas MacArthur's plea for U.S. missionaries to go to Japan. But that generation is now elderly, retiring from the front lines by the thousands.

What will be America's destiny in God's plan to penetrate the remaining unreached people groups of the world with bottom line blessings?

As the washing machine kicks in, you feel a little nervous about American Christians' preoccupation with top line blessings. You remember a church service you attended back in the winter of 1980 during the Iranian hostage crisis, when forty-two Americans were held hostage by terrorists in Teheran:

It's a bright Sunday morning outside the vaulted windows. You're seated comfortably among one of the largest fundamental, evangelical congregations in the USA. The morning service is smoothly orchestrated; you've relaxed in genuine meditative praise, enjoying a sweeping choral anthem in preparation for the biblical message. You glance at the order of service in the bulletin and see that Greg Livingstone, one of the founders of a fast-growing mission agency called Frontiers, is scheduled to give a "missions minute."

Right, you think. This guy's really going to be able to say something significant in sixty seconds. The one-minute missionary.

The anthem ends. A square man who looks like a boxer steps to the podium. Without so much as an introduction, he asks, "How many of you are praying for the fifty-two U.S. hostages held captive in Iran?"

You, of course, raise your hand. All present raised their hands. "Wow, that's terrific," he says. "There must be four thousand people here."

"Now, let's be just as honest; Jesus is watching. How

many of you," the boxer continues, "are praying for the 45 million Iranians held captive in Islam?"

One hand slowly goes up.   Two hands.

"What? Only two people?" he yells. "What are you guys, Americans first and believers second?" The ensuing silence is not smoothly orchestrated. It's a powerful sixty seconds you will never forget. He says, "And I thought this was a Bible-believing church!" and he sits down!

The Quiet Corner

In the last chapter, we touched on an idea that might be unfamiliar, maybe even a little uncomfortable to you: God loves other people groups just as intensely as He does His Chosen People. The Great Commission to reach out to those nations on God's heart is as old as Abraham.

How firmly entrenched is the Great Commission in the Old Testament? Let's face it: If the Great Commission is the solid theme of the Old Testament, if reaching all the nations has been God's priority since Genesis 12, then it needs to be the major theme, the driving force in our lives if we are to give God the maximum glory He should have.

If using His people to bless all the nations with the offer of redemption isn't really God's purpose for His church on the earth, then the whole enterprise of missions should be kept quietly in the corner of the narthex. To many of us, reaching the peoples of the world is a sideline compartment of Christianity. It's a bulletin board with fuzzy photos of couples and large families surrounding a faded map of the world, stuck here and there with blue and yellow pins. It's a once-a-year dutiful mission emphasis that leaves us feeling faintly guilty for how good we've got it. Missions mostly belongs to an obscure church committee whose main job is deciding how to allocate the funds that are routinely designated for reaching the world's ethnic groups, groups that aren't quite as important as we think we are.

The New Math

So, let's see if the Great Commission is actually foundational in the Old Testament. We'll begin with a closer look at the Tower of Babel. God instituted and created every one of the languages formed at the Tower of Babel, right? And if God created every one of those languages, we have to assume that God must have loved every one of those peoples equally, because He made them all, and their languages.

Now wait a minute. How does that last statement strike you?

Does God love every people group equally? Let's think this through, since it has tremendous implications as we consider the Great Commission in the Old Testament.

In Genesis 12, we found that the top line plus the bottom line equal His covenant. We could designate God's desire to bless Israel as "A," the top line. God's desire to bless all the nations can be "B," the bottom line. These equal His covenant, "C," His promise to Abraham.

So, we could say A + B = C, a simple mathematical equation. Any mathematician can tell us that A and B can have three possible relationships. A can be greater than B, A can be less than B, or A can be equal to B.

If A is greater than B, the Abrahamic promise is basically God saying this: "Look, Abraham, I want to bless you. I want to be your God. I want you to be My people. I want to pour out My Spirit and My love and my grace upon you because I love you. I want to do this because you are My chosen people and I am so infatuated with you. And if, Abraham, by chance, some of the blessing happens to spill out into all the Gentile groups,—Hey, that's no big deal. I can handle it. But right now, I want to bless you. My love for you is far greater than My love for all the nations."

That's "A is greater than B." Now, there are some verses which seem to back up that formula. In Deuteronomy 7:6 we find that God says, "I have chosen you, Israel, out of all the nations on the face of the earth to be my treasured possession." Now if God chose Israel out of all the nations on the face of the earth, that seems to say A is greater than B. God's love for Israel is greater than His love for all the nations. Do you agree?

Now, could A be less than B? Could God's love for the nations be far greater than His love for Israel? Well, frankly, no one ever assumes that. There's too much Scripture saying Israel is His treasured possession, the apple of His eye, etc.

So, the only other possible option that we have is that A is equal to B. If that is true, then what God basically said to Abraham was this, "Look, Abraham, I want to bless you. I want to pour out My grace and My mercy upon you. I want to be your God. I want you to be My people, and just as important, Abraham, I want that blessing to go to all the nations on the face of the earth. I want to reach every Gentile group because I love them equally." A equals B.

What will it be? A>B or A=B? Can you imagine Abraham scratching his head, wondering which one God meant?

Let's look at a passage of Scripture that will help shed some light on the question. "For I have chosen the Levite tribe out of all the tribes of Israel to stand

and minister in the Lord's presence always" (Deuteronomy
18:5). God chose the Levite tribe to stand and minister
in His name always.

There are twelve tribes. Notice the phrase "out of
all the tribes." Did God love the Levite tribe more than
He loved the other eleven tribes? No. But He had a
special purpose for the Levite tribe. Overlay that simple
concept on our understanding of Deuteronomy 7:6: "For
I have chosen you out of all the nations on the face of
the earth to be my treasured possession." Does this necessarily
mean God has a special love for Israel? Or, that He
has a special purpose for Israel? Let's try this on for
size: A=B. God has a special purpose for Israel and an
equal love for all nations.

As we'll see, whether we look at the world through
an A>B or through an A=B perspective can make a remarkable
difference in what we see. For example, if you have
an A>B perspective, what kind of a stance are you going
to take politically in the Middle East? You'll take a staunchly
pro-Israel stance. If you have an A=B perspective what
kind of a stance will you take politically? Justice for
all nations equally.

In the same way, our understanding of Scripture can
take a different twist if we begin to read it with an A
equals B perspective. We're finding that many theologians
have somehow been trained with an A is greater than
B perspective and that much of the teaching we get comes
from an A>B stance.

How about you? What kind of teaching have you been getting in your Christian upbringing?

Fill in the blank. "Be still and . . ." That's right, "know that I am God." Most Christians know that pretty well. That's because it refers to what part of the covenant? Of course, the top line. But how about the next half of the verse—do you know what it is?

"I will be exalted among the nations. I will be exalted in the earth." As we should have expected, the bottom line.

Most Christians can easily quote the beginning of Psalm 46:10, but they have no idea what the rest of the verse is. Why? They have been brought up under an A>B Christianity . . . Christianity that emphasizes how God has blessed us, but leaves off the bottom line responsibility "to be a blessing."

You will find it very interesting to think through many of the lessons you learned in Sunday school, growing up as a child. Most of the lessons you learned were probably top line lessons only—and you may have missed half of what the Bible is trying to tell you.

For example, think of Daniel in the lions' den. What lesson do we learn from Daniel in the lions' den? That's right: Trust in God, be faithful to Him and He will take care of you. What part of the covenant does that refer to? The top line. God wants to bless you. But is there a bottom line lesson to Daniel in the lions' den? You were probably never taught it in Sunday school, but the bottom line lesson is there.

Look at what King Darius does: "Then King Darius wrote to all the peoples, nations and men of every language throughout the land: 'May you prosper greatly! I issue a decree that in every part of my kingdom people must fear and reverence the God of Daniel'" (Daniel 6:25,26).

Here we have a Gentile king being used by the God of Israel to evangelize the Gentile world.

Think of it. You're a Gentile king who's been conquered by King Darius. You view him as the king of all kings, yet this king who conquered you is "Federal Expressing" you a letter telling you to worship and fear the God of Daniel—the Jews, a foreign people he's already conquered. What are you going to think? "Hey, that God of Israel must be pretty powerful. Isn't He the same God that they say brought about those plagues in Egypt and parted the Red Sea. And didn't He also..." Notice how committed God was in reaching out to all the peoples. "Then King Darius wrote to all the peoples, nations and men of every language..."

God can use your life to impact internationals around you, who will in turn, go and tell other internationals about your God. The bottom line lesson of Daniel in the Lion's Den.

David and Goliath is another example. What lesson is to be learned from David and Goliath? We wimps can take on giants. Right. Trust in God and we can take down all those bad guys—the top line lesson. Is there a bottom line?

Samuel 17:45-47. "David said to the Philistines, 'You come against me with sword and spear and javelin, but I come against you in the name of the Lord Almighty, the God of the armies of Israel, whom you have defied. This day the Lord will hand you over to me, and I'll strike you down and cut off your head. Today I will give the carcasses of the Philistine army to the birds of the air and beasts of the earth, and the whole world will know that there is a God in Israel.'"

How is the whole world going to know? That's right. Through merchants who, through their trading, would be bumping into a bunch of Philistines—running scared. "Why are they running scared?" they'd ask.

"That small boy just beat our giant."

Do you think they kept that secret to themselves? No! They passed it on from town to town, becoming human travelling newspapers spreading the news.

Who got the credit for that victory? Did David or the God of Israel? Yes, the God of Israel. With credit to Him for that victory, it was His reputation that began to be scattered to the very ends of the earth. Those traders would pass that story along everywhere they went, broadening the reputation of the God of Israel.

The plagues tell us the same thing. If you have an A>B perspective, what is God doing with the ten plagues? He is lording it over the Egyptians, showing His strength, causing them to fear Him . . . with no hope of knowing

Him.

If you have an A=B perspective, what is God doing? With this new perspective you would realize that each one of the plagues dealt with one of the gods of Egypt. As each plague occurred, the Egyptians would be seeing one of their gods knocked down. Of course they would begin to wonder, "Are we worshiping the true gods, or is the God of Israel greater?"

Look at the list below to see which gods were defeated.

THE TEN PLAGUES OF EXODUS

Plague	Passage	Egyptian gods defeated
#1 Nile	7:14-25	Osiris/Hapi and others
#2 Frogs	8:1-15	Heqt, frog, goddess of happiness
#3 Gnats/lice	8:16-19	Unnamed demigod related to priesthood
#4 Flies	8:20-32	Uatchit, the insect god
#5 Livestock	9:1-7	Sacred bulls, Hathor the cow goddess of love
#6 Boils	9:8-12	Imhotep, god of medicine
#7 Hail and fire	9:13-35	Nut, sky goddess
#8 Locusts	10:1-20	the locust god
#9 Darkness	10:21-29	Ra, (greatest of Egyptian gods) and many others
#10 Slaying of the first born	11:1-12:30	Pharaoh's son was said to be the son of god Amon-Re

Did any of the Egyptians come to the conclusion that the God of Israel was greater? Look at Exodus 12:38. "Many other people went up with them, as well as large droves of livestock, both flocks and herds." Who were those "other people?" That's right, Egyptians. Remember Psalm 87: "There will be Egyptians and Babylonians who acknowledge me." Continually God was reaching out to other peoples in the Old Testament through His miraculous work.

What about the Ten Commandments? Those were definitely top line, given to Israel to allow them to grow closer to Him and to walk in His holiness. Is there any bottom line in the Ten Commandments?

Look at Deuteronomy 4:6: "Observe them carefully, for this will show your wisdom and understanding to the nations, who will hear about all these decrees and say, 'Surely this great nation is a wise and understanding people.'"

When all the nations saw the great wisdom that there was in the Law, how were they going to respond? "Gee, great for them, sorry we can't apply it to ourselves." Or perhaps they would begin to say, "Your God has given you great wisdom and insight into His marvelous laws. Can we know your God?"

Even the Ten Commandments were to give wisdom not only to the Israelites themselves but to all the nations that would observe their laws. It was a testimony of the ways of the God of Israel.

Did you ever wonder why God gave Solomon such

wisdom? Yes, He wanted to bless Solomon and His people. He is a God who loves Israel. But it doesn't stop with the top line. There is a bottom line blessing to His wisdom.

Look at 11 Chronicles 9:22-23: "King Solomon was greater in riches and wisdom than all the other kings of the earth. All the kings of the earth sought audience with Solomon to hear what wisdom God had put in his heart."

As all these kings came from all over the earth to attend one of Solomon's "International Wisdom Seminars," do you think they learned about the God of Israel as well? You bet. And do you think he told them that the temple had a Gentile court? Yes, it was probably a vital part of Solomon's message to all of these kings.

It is this bottom line emphasis which probably was used by the Holy Spirit to determine which stories should be in the Scriptures. Did you realize . . .

Joseph was a blessing to the Egyptians (Genesis 41:4-7).

Moses had a Midianite convert - his father-in-law (Joshua 2:8-14).

Joshua and the spies were a blessing to Rahab of Jericho (Joshua 2:2-6).

Naomi was a blessing to Ruth of Moab (Ruth 2:12).

David reached out to the Gibeonites for the sake of the bottom line (2 Samuel 21:1-14).

Nathan rebuked David because he had put a Hittite to death (2 Samuel 12:9-14).

Solomon did some hard one-on-one evangelism to Queen Sheba (1 Kings 10:1-9).

The Temple had an outer court dedicated to Gentiles (1 Kings 42:43,60).

Elijah blessed the widow of Zarephath (1 Kings 17:7-24).

Elisha healed the commander of the army of the King of Aram--Naaman (2 Kings 5:1-26).

Jeremiah was a prophet to the nations (Jeremiah 1:5).

Daniel and his colleagues reached out to Nebuchad nezzar, an act that had international ramifications (Daniel 2:47-49; 3:28-29).

Jonah reached out to an entire Gentile city - Ninevah (Jonah 3:3-10).

God let the Ammonites know that He is Lord (Ezekiel 25:1-7), Moab too (5:8-11), Edom as well (25:12-14), the Philistines also (25:15-17), the people of Tyre (26:1-6), Sidon (28:20-24) and the nations (38:23).

God has given much "copy" to the Gentiles. Genesis 1-11 is non-Jewish, as well as the entire book of Job (written before Genesis 12 according to our best under-standing). That's fifty-three solid chapters right there.

Not only those, but all of Ruth, Esther, Obadiah, Jonah and Nahum have direct Gentile interaction. A third of the Psalms address the Gentiles positively! All of the Proverbs, Ecclesiastes and the Song of Solomon were written in a generic sense as if to all mankind. Who knows, they may have been the handouts at Solomon's "Internationl Wisdom" seminars!

Luke, a Gentile, wrote fifty-two solid chapters of the New Testament. Four of the five women mentioned in the lineage of Jesus Christ were Gentiles. Most of the letters written in the New Testament were to Gentiles.

Of course we don't need to go on. You're getting the picture. Large amounts of Scripture have been dedicated to the Gentiles—the peoples that God loves as much as His beloved Jerusalem.

Story after story in the Bible has both a top line message and a bottom line message. You may have been brought up learning only top line lessons, and as a result, you may have missed half of what the Bible is trying to tell you. Don't be discouraged. With this new perspective, you are going to see the Scriptures come alive as you see God's heart in a whole new way.

For Further Thought

To reinforce the concept of people groups' equality before God, write out an explanation of $A+B = C$, $A>B$ and $A=B$ as if to a child.

List other ideas new to you from this chapter's discussion.

List questions raised in this segment of study.

Scan the chapters, noting especially meaningful references and mark these in your personal study Bible.

Evaluate your life for any pronounced $A>B$ tendencies: Notice your prayer life, your calendar, your study of world news versus local or national news, your preparations for and dreams of the future.

Pray that Christians in America will be Christians first, Americans second.

Chapter 4

Discovering The Other Half Of Your Bible

You came back home from church a little shaken. Those sixty seconds were more powerful than the sermon itself. Are we really Americans first and Christians second?

Before you head out on your next trip, you need to spend some time with your little brother. He's missed you, and he's going to miss you more. So you nestle up beside him and begin to watch the "Sunday Singalong"— his favorite video tape. After three songs, a thought pops into your mind. "That's interesting. The last three songs dealt only with the top line of the covenant."

Reaching out for the box, you begin to scan over the songs and think through the words. Of the fourteen songs, only two of them deal with the bottom line. . . and you are being gracious in giving those two bottom line credit!

"Wow, is my little brother getting top line Christianity only?" your mind begins to wonder. How far does this infatuation with the top line of the covenant permeate our culture?

Later that day you turn on your radio to a Christian program and began to listen to the songs. With pen in hand, you are shocked. Ninety-five percent of the songs deal with the top line—God wants to bless you. There is little emphasis on the bottom line.

"Hey, let's push this further," you think. Getting in your '69 Volkswagen beetle, you head for the largest Christian bookstore in town. As you walk in, you spot the manager—an old high school friend who never went to to college but has proven to be business-wise. You head over there, and, after some small talk, you ask him what the majority of the books in his store deal with.

"That's an interesting question," he says. "Eighty-five percent of our books deal with how you can grow in your relationship with the Lord. We are really excited about that because we really believe in ministering to the saints."

"Where is the missions section?" you ask.

"Oh, it's over there, that bottom row of books in the corner." You walk in that direction and find that out of the 400-500 books in the entire store, fourteen deal with the bottom line. Are we so infatuated with ourselves that we have missed half of what the Bible is saying?

The clincher comes when he excitedly hands you a brochure on a conference that's coming up. "I wonder what type of teaching these people are going to get,"

you ask yourself as you hear his words trail away. ".
. . I hope you can be there. It's going to be a powerful conference" . . . . Top speakers from around the nation addressing the theme "To Run and Not Grow Weary." You check out the titles of the keynote addresses. . . all top line. You then read through the list of seminar electives and put a check by the bottom line titles: Two out of sixty.

We really are Americans first and Christians second, mostly due to the teaching we are getting. Are we so concerned for ourselves that we have missed the very heart of God?

Israel—A Great Commission Nation

Let's catch a fresh perspective on the Old Testament by viewing it from the A=B perspective. Remember, God wanted not only to bless Israel, but also to reach out to all the nations as well. So it should be no surprise to discover that the Old Testament is filled with references to the nations, the peoples, the Gentiles—all the people groups on earth other than the Israelites, as we saw in the last chapter.

Look back at Genesis 26:4 as the Abrahamic covenant is repeated to Isaac: "I will make your descendants as numerous as the stars in the sky and will give them all these lands, and through your offspring all nations on earth will be blessed."

Now, when we think about the stars in the sky, we

immediately think of top line lessons having to do with their number: Isaac will have thousands, millions, billions of descendants. But this imagery also has a secondary bottom line meaning. Stars shine. Isaac's descendants would be shining representatives of God to? . . . to all nations.

In tracing this recurring image through the Bible we learn God's people are to bring light to all people groups, all nations, all the Gentiles. Notice the obvious point of this metaphor in passages such as Simeon's prayer when the infant Jesus is presented in the Temple: "My eyes have seen your salvation . . . a light for revelation to the Gentiles" (Luke 2:30-31). Jesus, born through the chosen people of Israel, is the light of the Jews? Yes, but He's the light of the entire world of mankind.

Later, God repeats the covenant to Jacob with another twist of imagery. He says "Your descendants shall be like the dust of the earth" (Genesis 28:14). Now again, the image suggests the amazing number of Jacob's descendants. But there's more than just a top line lesson.

If you've ever traveled in the Middle East, you know all about dust. Actually, if you've ever cleaned house, you know dust; when it gets kicked up, it scatters all over. Jacob's descendants will be like the dust of the earth and "will spread out to the west and to the east and to the north and to the south." Do those phrases sound familiar?

Of course. We recognize them from Matthew 8, where

Jesus says there will be people from the north, the south, the east and the west who take their places at the feast with Abraham, Isaac and Jacob.

What is the result of their spreading out? Read the rest of Genesis 28:14: "All peoples on earth will be blessed through you and your offspring." All the nations will be "dusted" with God's blessing—the bottom line.

Dust doesn't form in a pile, nor do stars stay clumped together all over the sky.

God had a two-tiered strategy for world evangelization in the Old Testament. One strategy involved the central location of the Promised Land. The world's traders would come through Israel and take home the message of God's redemption. The nations would come to Israel, where His people would sparkle with the light of salvation.

This is seen in 1 Kings, Chapter 8. God had told

David that his son could build a temple to represent His name (see 1 Kings 5:3-5). Since that name represents the character of God, the Temple would portray to all onlookers who God is.

Notice how Solomon dedicates that temple: "As for the foreigner who does not belong to your people Israel but has come from a distant land because of your name— for men will hear of your great name and your mighty hand and your outstretched arm—when he comes and prays toward this temple, then, Lord, don't hear their prayer; make them green with envy because of the way you esteem us Jews."

A poor rendition, right? The passage doesn't say that at all. Solomon's dedicatory prayer petitions God in this way: ". . . men will hear of your great name and your mighty outstretched arm when he comes and prays towards this Temple, then hear from heaven, your dwelling place, and do whatever the foreigner asks of you, so that all the peoples of the earth may know your name and fear you, as do your own people Israel . . ." (1 Kings 8:41-43).

A equals B. This segment of Solomon's dedication was a bottom line prayer for those who would come to Jerusalem. In fact, for whom was the outer court of the Temple reserved? The Gentiles. This is another reason that Jesus was so upset in the New Testament when money changers were desecrating the Temple with their mer- chandising (see Mark 11:15-17). When non-Jews would come to the Temple after hearing about God's commitment to the Gentiles, what would be their impression of God if they found His house to be a den of thieves?

Basically, the money changers and the Temple overseers, who allowed their thievery, were making a statement: "These Gentiles are just dogs who are never going to know the Lord. Let's make this courtyard a marketplace and forget them." Jesus comes in,overturns their sleazy merchandising and says, "My house shall be called a house of prayer for all nations." So in 1 Kings 8 Solomon prays, "Lord, hear their prayer and answer that prayer." What would happen when God answered that foreigner's prayer? He would head home along the trade routes and testify, "The God of Israel answers the prayers of Gentile peoples!"

Those who listened to these reports would look at their idols and vow, "I'm going there. I want to find out about the God of the Jews." Remember Psalm 87: "There will be Egyptians and Babylonians and people from Tyre and Sidon of those who acknowledge me." God intended the Promised Land as a mission base to all the peoples of the world.

The Queen of Sheba, of course, represents the classic case of the world coming to the doorstep of God's people. Read through 1 Kings 10, and envision the spread of God's news of redemption and blessing as she and her retinue traveled back to Ethiopia. What did they and the traders they met talk about? The amazing message that—as far as the God of Israel was concerned—A equals B. That

God was as committed to blessing an Ethiopian as He was committed to a Jewish Solomon.

And the news spread over the miles and over the years, which is quite possibly why in Acts 8, an Ethiopian knew he could go up to that Temple to pray, that God had a special court reserved for all Gentiles. God's reputation had been established hundreds of years before, through Solomon's cross-cultural evangelism to the Queen of Sheba.

With an A=B perspective, the Old Testament comes alive with Gentiles being confronted with the God of Israel.

Dusty Missionaries

The second tier of God's Old Testament strategy to evangelize the world involved sending Israel as a missionary nation. Israel would go and infiltrate like dust or sand into every nook and cranny of the nations of the earth. The Genesis 28 imagery suggests the Great Commission in another form: "Go therefore, and make disciples of all nations. Spread out like the dust of the earth, and all nations north, south, east and west of you will be blessed."

Why is Israel commissioned to bless other nations? Because A = B. The most primitive tribe in the remote corner of the earth's wilderness was as important to God as the Chosen People. "God does not show favoritism" (see the context of Romans 2:11) between the Jews and any other people group on earth!

When we review old familiar stories of God's development

of Israel as a nation with an A = B attitude, we'll find there are dozens of examples of God's missionary mandate to the Hebrews.

Try to rethink the familiar events of the Exodus with an A = B perspective. The central point of the record, of course, has to do with what happens within the Israelite camp. But the heart of God is, as always, intent on reaching all peoples. For instance, imagine what goes on in Midian as Moses leads the Hebrews out of Egypt.

"Now Jethro, the priest of Midian and father-in-law of Moses, heard of everything God had done for Moses and for his people Israel, and how the Lord had brought Israel out of Egypt" (Exodus 8:1). Is Jethro, the priest of the Midianites, Jew or Gentile? Gentile. From quite a distance, he had heard of everything the Lord had done for Israel. How? Was Moses FAXing him? No. It was through the traders, those human travelling newspapers—the only way most of the world had of communicating. And what were they communicating?

Keep thinking through the context. There was no Old Testament world trade center that sent a memo out to all the eighteen-wheeler camels saying, "No one trade with Egypt. The God of the Hebrews is taking on the gods of the Egyptians, and it is unsafe. Once a victor arises, it will then be safe to resume trading."

They did trade. Just think of the conversation around the watering hole . . .

"Yeah, last time I got into Cairo, everything's covered

with flies! So I ask, 'What are all these flies doing here?' And they say, 'Oh, well, that's the God of the Hebrews defeating the gods of the Egyptians.' Wild days down there. What kind of a God covers a country with flies?"

Another trader pulls his camel up to the well and says, "Wow! I wish I had a surplus of frogs. You should have seen . . . !" Every watering hole they went to, they passed this new information on. What was the world talking about? The true, powerful God, the God of Israel. City after city heard these stories through those traveling sources of information and became impressed with the Lord.

As the entourage of Hebrews followed Moses to Mount Sinai, other events took place. God greatly protected His people. With an A>B perspective, you leave it at that. But with an A = B perspective, you're encouraged to view the old familiar story in a new light. Keep your imagination running for a few more minutes. With an A = B perspective, imagine the reaction of other people groups to God's leading Israel in their desert journey through the "pillar of cloud by day and the pillar of fire by night."

What happens in the desert during the day time? It gets incredibly hot. At night it gets incredibly cold. Everyone watching this exodus of two and a half million people, saw the pillar of cloud that came in the daytime. What did it do? It kept God's people cool. And the pillar of fire at night? It kept them warm.

Now, imagine—you're a Hivite. You're in the Promised

Land and you're looking to the horizon and you see a strange glow. You've seen it the past few evenings and you're curious. A trader comes by and you say, "Excuse me, sir, but could you tell me what that glow is on the horizon?"

He says, "Oh, that's the God of the Jews."

"The God of the Jews? They worship fire as a god?"

"No, He's a God that cannot be seen. He's the God of the heaven and the earth, they say, and they have many names for Him." And the trader would list the names he had heard—God as Provider, God the All-Nourishing One, etc. He adds, "So their God is protecting His people in the desert."

You're really curious now. "He's protecting them in the desert?"

"Yes, He keeps them warm at nighttime with a huge pillar of fire, and He keeps them cool during the day with a cloud. You've seen those big clouds over there all day? That's Him, keeping them cooled off, protecting them during the day."

"Well, how do all of those people eat?" you ask.

"You're not going to believe it, but it's miraculous. I've seen it myself. Bread comes down out of heaven; they call it manna."

"Excuse me," you interrupt. "Is that the same God that sent all those plagues in Egypt that I heard about?"

"Yep, the same one."

"Is it the same one who brought them through the

Red Sea on dry land?" you continue.

"Yep, same God."

"Wow!" Your mind races as you say, "Thank you very much, sir. I've been wondering for so long . . . it's kind of strange though, it's been going around in circles for so long . . ." You turn and gaze at that glow over the horizon. Then you turn around and frown at a little piece of wood plated with gold, the thing your uncle made that you bow down to and you call your god. You say, "You know what, you haven't done much for me lately. In fact, you haven't done anything for me lately!"

And you look out again and watch the glow. You might easily say in your heart of hearts, "God, if I can know You, I want to know You."

Do you think the God of Israel would listen to that Hivite's prayer? Probably not if A is greater than B. But if A equals B, that is exactly the prayer God would be listening for. God reached out to other nations by establishing a reputation for Himself through the Chosen People.

God even used Israel's military maneuvers to broadcast His love for all peoples. Although there are dozens of examples, let's consider one of the first forays the Israelites made into the Promised Land against the city of Jericho.

The fact that God was giving miraculous victory to Israel was striking truth to the hearts of Canaanites. Listen to Jericho's famous prostitute Rahab as she responds to the bottom line of the Abrahamic promise: "I know that the Lord has given this land to you and that a great fear of you has fallen on us, so that all who live in this country are melting in fear because of you. We have heard how the Lord dried up the water of the Red Sea for you when you came out of Egypt" (Joshua 2:8-10a).

How did they hear? From traders who saw the Egyptians wash up dead on the shore. Rahab continues: "And what you did to Sihon and Og, the two kings of the Amorites east of the Jordan, whom you completely destroyed. When we heard of it, our hearts sank and everyone's courage failed because of you, for the Lord your God is the God in heaven above and on the earth below" (Joshua 2:10b-11).

Did she know that the God of Israel was the true and living God? Will we find her in heaven because the military victories of God's people forced her to reckon with the true God? Yes, we will. In fact, notice the references in the New Testament to this Gentile's faith in God (see Matthew 1:5, Hebrews 11:31 and James 2:25). You'll find a prostitute, a resident of Israel's enemy Jericho, extolled right along with Abraham as an example of faith in God's redemption.

Now you might be saying, "Hey, wait a second, how can A equal B if God had all those nations destroyed?" Good question. But there is an answer in the following chapters. Hold on!

How firmly entrenched was the Great Commission in the Old Testament? Notice that before giving the Law, God announces to Israel: "Now if you obey me fully and keep my covenant, then out of all nations you will be my treasured possession. Although the whole earth is mine, you will be for me a kingdom of priests and a holy nation" (Exodus 19:5).

The phrase, "fully keep my covenant," refers to what covenant? The promise to Abraham, Isaac and Jacob. Obeying and fully keeping His covenant will involve an amazing responsibility for this people group: "You will be for me a kingdom of priests."

What do priests do? They intercede for the sins of the people (Hebrews 5:1). Now if these Israelites were to be a whole kingdom of priests, what were they to do? Were all of the Jews with last names beginning with A-M to be priests for all those Jews whose last names began with N-Z, every Tuesday, Thursday and Saturday? And then were they rotated responsibilities every Monday, Wednesday and Sunday?

Not quite. Have you ever seriously considered God's intention for making an entire people a "kingdom of priests"? If God's people are to be a kingdom of priests, for whom were they to be priests? Themselves only?

We know better. Since God loves all peoples equally, since A equals B, Israel was to serve as a kingdom of priests for the nations.

Is the Task Do-able?
Is it obvious yet? God designated Israel to shine and spread the Great Commission news of God's blessing. Before

we look at the obvious question of the Israelites' success at being Great Commissioners, let's look at another question.

Was it practically possible for the children of Israel to accomplish this purpose? In the beginning, Abraham and his descendents giving a message to sixty-nine other groups doesn't seem like too ridiculous a task. But some statisticians suggest that by the time of Christ, those seventy groups had splintered into approximately 60,000 distinct people groups!

How could the little nation of Israel, struggling simply to survive, ever hope to mount a realistic campaign of reaching that many other peoples with the message of God's blessing?

Perhaps you feel that way today about the Great Commission. It's a big world out there; there are more than five billion persons. With more coming all the time in alarming, exponential population growth. And most of that growth is precisely in the regions of the earth least penetrated by the light of salvation.

For example, a people group you've probably never heard of is the Orizaba nation in the Mexican state of Veracruz. Think of 50,000 individuals, the direct modern descendents of the ancient Aztecs, with no knowledge of the blessings of redemption offered in Christ. Think of them dedicating their children to the spirits in hope of receiving blessing.

They're animists—spirit worshipers—with beliefs that are perversions of Roman Catholicism. They speak Nahuatl, not Spanish. Mission groups' attempts to reach them with the Gospel have largely been met with disturbing accounts of spiritual attack. Over the past thirty years, for example, a major mission agency has had missionary after missionary return from that field with a broken family, broken health and disillusionment.

The Orizaba have been bound in the kingdom of darkness since the pre-history of the Aztecs. And you're commanded to reach them.

Before you become too deeply discouraged, think through the astounding implications of a few lines from the beautiful song of Moses:

> Remember the days of old;
> Consider the generations long past.
> Ask your father and he will tell you,
> Your elders, and they will explain to you.
> When the Most High gave the nations their inheritance,
> When he divided all mankind,
> He set up boundaries for the peoples
> according to the number
> of the sons of Israel.
> (Deuteronomy 32:7-8).

Interesting lyrics, aren't they? Why would God be diligent to set up the boundaries for all the nations in direct proportion to the numbers of the sons of Israel?

The proportion could be geographical—limits to territorial domain. That is, as the people groups began to broaden and gain new territory on the face of the earth,

God allowed Israel to grow larger geographically as well.

Or the proportion could be numerical boundaries—limits to population. Perhaps God determined the population growth of each people group according to the future population growth of the Hebrews. Perhaps He determined how many distinct people groups there would be on the earth in direct proportion to the number of the Jews.

Whether referring to geographical or numerical factors, the meaning of the statement is clear: God has set the boundaries of the nations in direct proportion to the number of the sons of Israel.

And the point is this: If revival had ever broken out among the Jews, if they had caught the vision of reaching every people group for God, they would have been able to do it. Their Great Commission was practical, possible. God's plan wouldn't allow the proportion of the number of His people per unreached people group to get out of hand.

The Great Commission, God determined, would be a realistic task that could be accomplished.

Later in our study, you may be a bit astounded to find what the proportion of today's churches and evangelical Christians is to the people groups yet to be reached with the news of God's blessing. Is the Great Commission still practical, still possible?

Go Ye

Was Israel really commanded to reach all the people

groups of the world? Even though we don't see the eager obedience of Abraham, Isaac and Jacob's descendants actually going out to the Gentiles, we must not assume that this is proof that God did not want them to go. More likely we must conclude that this is evidence of their disobedience.

The Word clearly states, "Say among the nations, 'The Lord reigns'" (Psalm 96:10).

Did the Israelites ever realize how poor their performance was in obeying that command? The Apostle Paul in New Testament times quotes Old Testament passages such as Ezekiel 36:22 and writes that God's name is blasphemed among the Gentiles because of "you who call yourself Jews" (Romans 2:24).

It seems that God's people should have clearly seen the seriousness of disobeying the Abrahamic covenant's bottom line responsibility. But somehow, few of them felt the sting of their nation's dismal history of disobedience as acutely as the prophet Isaiah. Listen to his heartfelt lament:

> As a woman with child and about to give birth
> writhes and cries out in her pain,
> so were we in your presence, O Lord.
> We were with child, we writhed in pain,
> but we gave birth to wind.
> We have not brought salvation to the earth;
> we have not given birth to the people of the world.
> (Isaiah 26:17-18)

Same Treatment

A does equal B. It makes sense then that God would treat other nations equally.   For example:

We all know that the Jews were sent into seventy years of captivity.   But did you know Egypt was sent into forty years of captivity as well?   (Ex.29:13).   Tyre was sent into seventy years of captivity (Isaiah 3:9).

God says the nations are just like Israel: "Are not you Israelites that came to me as the Cushites?" declares the Lord. "Did I not bring Israel up from Egypt, the Philistines from Caphtor and the Arameans from Kir?" (Amos 9:7).

Why don't we have a record of all the direct dealings of God working with the other nations in the canon of Scripture?

A simple answer might be that if we had all of the writings of how God dealt with all the other nations on the face of the earth, God's canon of Scripture would weigh more than a cannon!

So with its concentration on God's dealings with His selected people group, the Old Testament is, unfortunately, easily read with an A>B perspective.   That's the stance even the prophet Jonah took as he ironically resented God's love for the repentant city of Nineveh (see Jonah 1-4).

What difference does A=B instead of A>B make in God's economy?   Think of it this way: If A is greater than B, then God's people can and should concentrate on their own welfare, their own growth and comfort, since they're more beloved to God than any other people on the globe.

Their prayers should rightly resound with pleas for more of God's blessing, with complaints about how unfairly they're being cared for as the world's prime-A people, for cries for Him to ease any of their suffering regardless of the suffering of others. It is of no great consequence if they don't get around to passing on bottom line blessings, since no other group is really quite as deserving as they are of God's love.

On the other hand, if A equals B, the entire picture changes.

Those "A people" who are blessed with top line blessings are fortunate not because they're better than any other group; they're blessed first simply because of God's sovereign selection. And since other groups equally deserve God's blessing, the "A's" are obligated to share God's blessings.

Selah is one of those wonderful Hebrew terms used often in the Psalms that suggests we pause and meditate on how a passage applies to our own lives. So read through those last couple of paragraphs; and selah.

What was God's reaction to Israel's poor performance record of following the Great Commission of Genesis 12? As we'll see in our next section of study, He mercifully sent them blindness!

For Further Thought

For individual and small group study:

Do some further study on how God used unusual missionary methods to spread the good news of His blessing of redemption:

He allowed the slavery of a little girl to reach a Gentile in graphic example of A=B. See 1 Kings 5:1-20.

He orchestrated events so that the Gentile king of Assyria commissioned Israeli priests to go as missionaries to Gentile settlers in Samaria! See 2 Kings 17:24-28.

With an A=B perspective, review several of your favorite Old Testament stories to consider how the nations might respond to God's dealings with Israel.

Explain some of the new A=B perspective you've discovered in this chapter to a friend who may not know the bottom line lessons.

Go to Appendix D and look over a comparison of two churches (both theoretical) and their persepctive towards missions. Place a check mark by which charater-istic is seen in your church.

Pray that the Chinese church would catch a vision for the thirty to fifty million Muslims in Northwest China who are virtually being untouched.

Chapter 5

God's Mercy Through Blindness

You're traveling again. Somehow your clothes got cleaned just in time to stuff them back into a suitcase. You're trying to catch a global perspective on God's orchestration of what many are calling the final era of the Great Commission.

Your 747 begins to descend over Bolivia.

Your flight from Miami to La Paz has been uneventful, so you had plenty of time to review your notes:

    Africa—50% Christian by AD 2000

        Unreached people groups: several hundred Muslim groups and thousands of small tribals. Progress good.

    North America—70 million evangelicals

        Dozens of unreached people groups of American Indians within its borders.

You jot a question to yourself as you descend: Is America obedient to the mandate? Are those totally untargeted Indian tribes indications of America's cross-eyed preoccupation with the top line? If so, how long till serious judgment? Or is it happening already?

You remember in your journeys across Africa and travel in Europe, how often you heard Christianity denounced as decadent and meaningless. Why? Because the only contact millions across the world have with what they think is Christianity from "Christian" America is Dallas, Halloween III and Madonna. What has America done with the Name of God among the nations?

The "fasten your seat belts" announcement crackles over the jet's loudspeaker in Spanish and English.

You glance quickly at your notes on South America's role in God's ultimate purpose.

> Brazil—evangelicals attending church now outnumber Roman Catholics attending mass.
>
> Brazil is now sending more than 1,000 missionaries.
>
> Moravian missionaries in Surinam now bringing people to Christ with the expressed stipulation that they have a part in reaching unreached people groups, particularly Muslims.
>
> Continent-wide, a whole new generation of believers supporting themselves as ministers, teachers and laborers. Students, serving as "inside advocates," help in their own people groups and are penetrating as never before into others' Christo-pagan and animistic cultures in courageous, no-holds-barred missions.
>
> God's reputation across the continent—?

You're landing, and you stuff away your notes, still worried about that last entry. Since the era of the Conquistadors, how has God's holy Name fared among the peoples of South America?

You deplane and walk stiffly among the European and Indian faces into the disinfectant smell, the here-and-there blasts of air conditioning of the La Paz airport corridors. And you immediately find the answer to your question by glancing at a discarded newspaper as you wait in line for customs.

The headlines shout: "Murder, Suicide Among Evangelicals!" The article hits only the melodramatic points of the incident.

A rural congregation in the Beni area of Bolivia, a group that identified itself as "evangelical Christian," held four days of prayer, fasting and dancing to purify their church. On the fourth day, the group began some sort of ritual to cast out demons. Here the news report gets fuzzy.

In the ensuing helter-skelter of frenzy, six people were either killed or committed suicide. Local and national authorities are now investigating, trying to find out from the surviving evangelical fanatics just what took place.

The article reports an intense public reaction: newspapers, TV, marketplace flyers all blame the evangelical community. Especially intense is retaliation against foreign evangelical missionaries; most report threats of violence. Certain leaders of a national evangelical association were detained by INTERPOL, the international police. The Bolivian government used the occasion to reactivate an old law which requires all non-Roman Catholic religious groups to get permits for all meetings in churches and homes. They must register all members and submit detailed financial records to the government. "Evangelical believer" is suddenly a term associated with the Peoples Temple—Jim Jones massacre in Guyana, an incident in the 70s—another South American incident that sullied the Name of God.

Waiting in line for your La Paz airport customs inspection, you feel nervous, conspicuous—as if you have "North American Evangelical" stamped across your passport. You're struck by how easily—with a little help from those who call themselves believers—the enemy can blind the minds of the nations to the claims of Christ by tarnishing the reputation of the God of the universe.

God's Mercy Through Blindness

Did the Israelites know they were supposed to reach out to the nations? It's probably pretty obvious through our study so far that the Great Commission was solidly established in the Old Testament. The Israelites were obviously mandated to share God's blessing with every people group on the face of the globe. Agree?

Why, then, does the Apostle Paul seem to disagree with us?

Paul describes this idea of the Gentiles coming into the kingdom as a mystery, as something not understood by the Jewish nation. What does Paul mean by this? We'd better study this through!

The Mystery

Paul writes in Ephesians 3:2-6: "Surely you have heard about the administration of God's grace that was given to me for you, that is, the mystery made known to me by revelation, as I have already written briefly. In reading this, then, you will be able to understand my insight into the mystery of Christ, which was not made known to men in other generations as it has now been revealed by the Spirit to God's holy apostles and prophets. This mystery is that through the Gospel the Gentiles are heirs together with Israel, members together of one body, and sharers together in the promise in Christ Jesus."

Paul is saying that there's been a mystery hidden for generations, and it's only now being understood. What is this mystery? This mystery is that the Gentiles are "heirs together with Israel."

Let's look further at what we thought was so obvious in even a cursory study of the Old Testament. In Romans 16, Paul closes his letter to the Romans with a prayer of praise: "Now to him who is able to establish you by my gospel and the proclamation of Jesus Christ, according to the revelation of the mystery hidden for long ages past, but now revealed and made known through the prophetic writings by the command of the eternal God, so that all nations might believe and obey him . . . .

There it is, the mystery hidden for long ages past, but now revealed.

Turn to Colossians 1:25-26 where Paul says, "I have become the church's servant by the commission God gave me to present to you the word of God in its fullness—the mystery that has been kept hidden for ages and generations, but is now disclosed to the saints.   To them God has chosen to make known among the Gentiles the glorious riches of this mystery, which is Christ in you, the hope of glory."

Here we see that there are two parts to this mystery: (a) that the Gentiles can know salvation, and   (b) that the Spirit of Christ can actually be in you.

The second part of the mystery is pretty familiar to us.   Why?

Could it be that it relates firmly to a top line blessing? Throughout the Old Testament there is a wonderful emphasis on the promise that God is with you.   Sometime when you're ready for an especially powerful Bible study, get a good exhaustive concordance and follow the references to "God is with you" in the Old Testament.   But when we come to the New Testament, we find a whole new understanding of God's relation to His people with the revelation that God is in you, not just with you.

The first part of the mystery—that the Gentiles are heirs together with Israel—isn't quite such a familiar study to us and seemed to be big news to Paul's Jewish audiences.

Paul flatly says that this has been a mystery hidden

for ages—even though we clearly saw it in our study through the Old Testament! Something is wrong here in light of our new A = B understanding. Let's find out what it is.

Look back at Colossians 1:25. Notice the phrase "the word of God in its fullness." What is Paul referring to here, the New or the Old Testament? Clearly it has to be the Old. That means that what Paul is saying is that this mystery has been there all the time (in the Old Testament), we just haven't understood it.

Notice also the phrase, "more fully." Paul is also saying that all of the teaching that they have had up until this time from their rabbis has been incomplete. (Maybe it came from an A>B perspective?) And now what Paul is going to give them is going to fill in the rest of the story—"Page Two," as Paul Harvey would say.

Let's skip down to Ephesians 3:8-9: "Although I am less than the least of all God's people, this grace was given me: to preach to the Gentiles the unsearchable riches of Christ, and to make plain to everyone the administration of this mystery, which for ages past was kept hidden in God." Notice that interesting phrase "which for ages past was kept hidden in God."

Now for a couple of questions: If God actually chooses to hide something, who can understand it? Can anybody? And another question:

Why would God put something into a culture and not immediately reveal its meaning? Or, getting back to our Bible study, why would God put something in the Old Testament Scriptures, yet not reveal it?

It's a good question, one that requires a little digging for the clear, surprising answer. Let's begin by digging back in, of course, the Old Testament.

Foundations

In order to fully understand why God would put something in the Scriptures and not reveal its meaning, we need to lay two simple foundations.

The first is that God knows of our future disobedience, just as He knew in Deuteronomy 31 of Israel's future disobedience to His commandments:

And the Lord said to Moses: "You are going to rest with your fathers, and these people will soon prostitute themselves to the foreign gods of the land they are entering. They will forsake me and break the covenant I made with them. On that day I will become angry with them and forsake them; I will hide my face from them, and they will be destroyed. Many disasters and difficulties will come upon them. . ." (Deuteronomy 31:16-17).

A second foundation is found in the story of Moses' defense of Israel before God. Remember the context. Moses has gone up into the Glory of the Lord, which is like a consuming fire. After two or three weeks, most Israelites probably think he is dead.

They then turn to Aaron and say, "Aaron, make us a god." They melt down their gold, and later, out pops a calf from the fire. At this point God directs this to the attention of Moses, telling of their impending judgment.

"Then the Lord said to Moses, 'Go down, because your people, whom you brought up out of Egypt, have become corrupt. They have been quick to turn away from what I commanded them and have made themselves an idol cast in the shape of a calf. They have bowed down to it and sacrificed to it and have said, "These are your gods, O Israel, who brought you up out of Egypt."'

"I have seen these people," the Lord said to Moses, "and they are a stiff-necked people. Now leave me alone so that my anger may burn against them and that I may destroy them. Then I will make you into a great nation." But Moses sought the favor of the Lord his God. "O Lord," he said, "why should your anger burn against your people, whom you brought out of Egypt with great power and a mighty hand?" (Exodus 32:7-11)

Notice below what Moses says about the consequences should God destroy Israel for its unfaithfulness to Him:

"Lord, why should your anger burn against your people, whom you brought out of Egypt with great power and a mighty hand? Why should the Egyptians say, 'It was with evil intent that he brought them out, to kill them in the mountains and to wipe them off the face of the earth'? Turn from your fierce anger; relent and do not bring disaster on your people. Remember your servants Abraham, Isaac and Israel, to whom you swore by your own self: 'I will make your descendants as numerous as the stars in the sky and I will give your descendants all this land I promised them, and it will be their inheritance forever.'" Then the Lord relented and did not bring on his people the disaster he had threatened" (Exodus 32:11-14).

Ultimate Courtroom Drama

What is happening here? To put in today's terminology, Moses basically appoints himself defense attorney for two and a half million of his own people down there at the foot of the mountain. Now, as a defense attorney, he's got a tremendous challenge facing him, because the prosecuting attorney happens to be the living God.

To complicate matters a thousand times, the Judge also happens to be the living God. If Moses can win this case in court, he should be acclaimed as the greatest lawyer of all time, and every lawyer should have to study this passage to see how he did it. This is high drama in the ultimate courtroom!

What does Moses do? Like any good attorney for the defense, he begins to listen to every word of the prosecuting attorney to find out whether there is some little foothold, some leverage to break open his case.

Listening intently, he catches a few crucial words. What are those words? Look back at the passage to see if you notice what Moses did about God's statements.

Look at verse nine. God mentions that He will make of Moses "a great nation." Sound familiar? It sounds familiar to Moses, too, as his mind pours over previous documents that might have a bearing on the case. "I will make you into a great nation" refers to what part of the covenant? The top line.

In effect, Moses says, "Surely, Lord, if you're interested in the top line of the covenant, you must be interested in the bottom line as well." Therefore, as the wise defense attorney, he begins to talk about the Egyptians. Now, let's think through that. Why would Moses begin to talk about the Egyptians in referring to the bottom line of the covenant?

Well, let's suppose that you're an Egyptian. You're in the pre-exile days. You've been enjoying a good, comfortable, secure life. You've got your family. Your kids are in a great Pharaonic school. You've got a nice job. Things are working out pretty well for you. You've got Hebrews as slaves. The women come in and take care of your home and sing songs to your little ones about some legendary God of Abraham, Isaac and Jacob. The men are baking bricks and building on an extra bedroom addition to your house.

All of a sudden, a man comes out of the desert st-u-u-u-tuttering. (You would stutter, too, if all you had heard was "ba-a-a-a-a" for forty years.) This character demands an audience with Pharoah and says, "Let my people go!"

Well, you don't think very much of him—he's not too impressive. He does a little miracle with power he says comes from the invisible, living and true God of Israel. Your magicians do the same miracle—and his snake eats their snake. You get a little worried, but there's plenty of magic you don't understand. Then as time goes on, another miracle happens. Your magicians match it. Another miracle. They match that. Just magic, right?

A fourth miracle and you hear that the magicians are beginning to worry. A fifth miracle. A sixth miracle. Things your magicians can't even touch.

All of a sudden the Egyptian magicians are saying to the Pharaoh, "This has to be from the finger of God. We're not even coming close to matching what He can do."

Now, if you're a sincere seeker and really want to know truth, what must be going through your mind is,

"Am I worshipping the right gods? The highest, most powerful gods? Or is this God of Israel really the true God? And if He is, maybe I should go out into the desert with these Hebrews."

Like any human, you don't want to waste your life on a lie; you want truth and reality. And if you're worshiping false gods or lesser gods, you're living out a lie. Maybe you ought to break down and follow the Israelites out into the desert to meet this true God.

But you're still borderline. You're not sure. You've got all this comfort, all this security. Why throw it all away? So you're wrestling: Do I or don't I? Another miracle happens. And a final supernatural blow brings the impact of this amazing God into your living room— every firstborn son in Egypt is miraculously slain. Including yours. Including the Pharaoh's son, and Pharaoh was supposed to be such a powerful god. This God of the Hebrews has finally gotten your undivided attention; the streets echo with wails of grief and terror. This is a God to be reckoned with, to be seriously worshiped before He decides to show more of His power.

Then the next morning you wake up and the Hebrews are gone. They've gone out into the desert. Yet in the market you hear that Pharaoh is going out to get the Hebrew people back, and you think: This is it. It's our god, the supreme Pharoah against this invisible God of the Hebrews. Now there's going to be some resolution in your mind about which gods or God to follow.

That evening the streets are clamoring with the news: The Pharoah is dead! The Hebrews passed through the sea on dry land! Miracle of miracles! Then the waters closed on Pharaoh and all his chariots!

In the craziness and the grief of these recent events, you're almost forced to think: I'd better find out about this God of the Hebrews and start worshiping Him. Maybe I can catch a ship across the sea and still catch up with them. But I've got all this security, my position and lifestyle, everything that's kept me comfortable here at home. Should I go worship the God of Israel? Should I leave all this for what I now know is the truth?

Unfortunately, it's a predicament many Christians find themselves in today. Do I leave comfort and security and head out-figuratively or perhaps literally-into the unknown desert of Lordship to follow after God?

You, the Exodus-era Egyptian, wrestle with it. The turmoil is welling up inside you. Well, one morning you get up out of bed, stagger past your firstborn son's empty bedroom. You're grief-stricken, miserable. You couldn't sleep as you wrestled with your conscience . . . Should I go, should I stay . . . go . . . stay? You grab your cup of Sanka. You step out into the sunlight and pick up the Cairo Daily News. You open it up and are struck with the headline: GOD OF ISRAEL DESTROYS HIS 2 1/2 MILLION FOLLOWERS!

Have you just now decided whether or not you'd

like to follow the God of the Hebrews? Of course. Your answer is "No way!" If one's God blesses like that, who needs enemies?

And as the headlines spread across the trade routes to eventually reach all the other nations on the face of the earth, whose reputation would be destroyed? God's. And if God's reputation is destroyed, would many of these people groups He is calling to Himself respond? No way! Therefore, He could not fulfill the bottom line of the covenant and He'd be called a liar for all of eternity.

That is defense attorney Moses' argument.

But Moses sought the favor of the Lord his God. "O Lord," he said, "why should your anger burn against your people, whom you brought out of Egypt with great power and a mighty hand? Why should the Egyptians say, 'It was with evil intent that he brought them out, to kill them . . . and wipe them off the face of the earth'?"

In other words: Lord, your reputation is going to be ruined; I know we're a worthless mob and deserve extinction, but how could the Egyptians trust you, if you wipe us out (not to mention that other nations won't be interested in following you either)? "Turn from your fierce anger; relent and do not bring disaster on your people. Remember your servants Abraham, Isaac and Israel" (Exodus 32:11-23).

What is Moses referring to? The Abrahamic covenant, naturally.

God's reputation, His Name, cannot be profaned among

the nations—not because God has a fragile ego, but because they'll turn away from Him and this would not allow His bottom line to be fulfilled.

With the realization of how crucial it is to keep God's reputation in good standing to fulfill the bottom line of the covenant, let's look at Ezekiel 20:13-14. Here, God is reviewing Israel's track record of following Him, making specific reference to the golden calf incident we just studied.

"Yet the people of Israel rebelled against me in the desert. They did not follow my decrees . . . So I said I would pour out my wrath on them and destroy them in the desert. But for the sake of my name, I did what would keep it from being profaned in the eyes of the nations in whose sight I had brought them out."

"But for the sake of my name." Another way of saying that is "for the sake of His reputation." God wanted to protect His reputation in the sight of the nations who had seen Him bring Israel out. Why was He concerned about His reputation in the eyes of the nations? Of course, because they were to be the fulfillment of the bottom line of the covenant.

Therefore, what did God do?

Further on in a strikingly similar statement about Israel's later disobedience, God does announce His corrective judgment of dispersing them "among the nations and scatter them through the countries" (in Ezekiel 20:21-26). But here God simply states that He did what would keep His reputation from being profaned among the nations. What was that "what"?

In order to understand what that "what" was, we need to think a minute about a fine American pastime: guilt.

Guilt is solely a matter of what you do, or do not do, before God. True or false? You're right, it's a false statement. Guilt is not merely a matter of what you do, or do not do, before God, but what you do, or do not do, in light of what you know. Of the one to whom much has been given, much is required.

Let's develop a diagram to clarify this. We'll start out with an arrow representing man's disobedience. As man progresses from the left to the right in time, he's getting more and more disobedient.

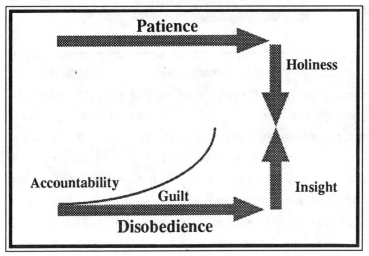

Accountability is determined by the combination of what he does and what he knows.

Paralleling disobedience is another line representing God's patience toward man's sin. As man's disobedience increases, God is patient. Yet even though unlimited in patience, He does act out of holiness, in His hatred of sin. That's the descending vertical line.

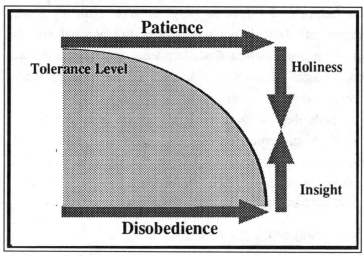

These two form another curve: God's tolerance level. This suggests how much sin God will tolerate. Now it's possible that a certain point can come at which man's accountability/guilt line and God's tolerance line intersect. It's as if God says at this point, "I've had it with your sin. I'm patient, but out of My holiness and out of my hatred of sin, I must act." This of course, is when man's accountability hits God's tolerance level. We'll call it judgment.

Think of some examples of judgment in the Old Testament. Sodom and Gomorrah. Korah's rebellion. In the New Testament, Ananias and Sapphira's lie.

Now try plotting those examples on your own graph. Plot the extremely low insight but tremendous disobedience of Sodom and Gomorrah. God's judgment finally struck after quite a long time of disobedience.

If you plotted a nearly vertical line that intersected quickly with the line of God's tolerance, could it represent Moses' judgment? His insight was tremendous, and his disobedience in striking a rock seems minimal. But still, God's action in judgment strikes, and Moses pays the consequences by not being allowed to enter the Promised Land.

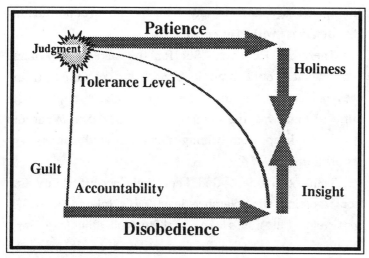

Notice that this judgment is not necessarily a question of going to heaven or to hell. Judgment is more often a practical consequence, a "reaping of destruction" (see Galatians 6:7), including physical death—being taken out of the game called life.

But let's sum up the point of the chart: There comes a point when man's accountability can cross God's tolerance level, and then comes judgment, when God will act out of His hatred of sin.

Now let's look back to Ezekiel 20:13. ". . . I said I would pour out my wrath on them and destroy them in the desert." What does that sound like? Israel's guilt line was soon going to cross God's tolerance level, and He was going to bring about a judgment. But if God did judge, what would happen? He'd ruin His reputation and never be able to fulfill the bottom line of the covenant among the Egyptians or any other people group watching His dealings with His people.

Therefore He says, "But for the sake of my name I did what would keep it from being profaned in the eyes of the nations in whose sight I had brought them out." What was the "what" that God did? What did He do to keep from wiping them out and ruining His reputation?

Think carefully. God kept their accountability line from crossing His tolerance level. His tolerance level is consistent, but man's accountability/guilt line can vary. In what way? The guilt line, we've seen, is made up of two components: insight and disobedience. This may be new material to you, so stick with the concept.

Which is the "easiest" for God to manipulate? Insight, which is what God reveals, or disobedience, which is based on man's decisions?

The answer is insight.

So let's propose that God brought over His people a cloud of blindness, a spiritual blindness so that they did not understand the Scriptures fully. And in not understanding the Scriptures fully, they were less accountable in their disobedience. Remember, just as of the one to whom much has been given, much is required, the converse also holds true, of the one to whom less has been given, less is required.

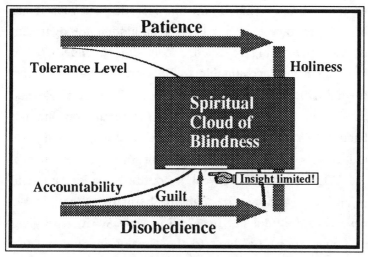

As Israel's accountability curve was rising and would soon intersect with God's tolerance line in judgment, God blinded their insight. He blinded them from understanding part of the Scriptures, to keep them less accountable, so as to not bring about judgment, and to be able to attract people from other nations to Him and fulfill the bottom line of the covenant.

Now, to what part of the Scriptures do you think God made them blind? Into what two components can all of the Scriptures be divided? Top line and bottom line components. (Remember Jesus at the Upper-Room Seminar?)

Back to the Israelites' blindness. What part of the covenant do you think God would blind them to?

The bottom line of the covenant. He blinded them from understanding their responsibility to reach out to all the nations. This is why the Apostle Paul says it has been a mystery that has been kept hidden for ages, but is only now being revealed. Why did He hide it? To keep them less accountable so He wouldn't have to judge them in the sight of all the nations. Because if He had done that, He would have ruined His reputation and not been able to fulfill the bottom line of the covenant. He did this because He knew of their future disobedience.

Why would God reveal it to the Apostle Paul, and to us now, and not to them back then? What do we have that they did not have? The Holy Spirit, who gives us power to be obedient to the Great Commission (Acts 1:8) (to keep us on the left side of the graph).

And so God in His great mercy blinded them! The Israelites' minds were made dull as if covered with a veil. It has not been removed, because only in Christ is it taken away. Even to this day when Moses is read, a veil covers their hearts (2 Corinthians 3:14-15).

God knows our future obedience—yes, yours too. He's

giving us insight into understanding the true, big picture of the Great Commission. If He knows that our future disobedience is there, He'll blind us into understanding the Great Commission, and we'll be less responsible for it, so that He won't have to judge us here on this earth in light of our insight.

You say, "Yes, it's a great graph, but prove it biblically."

Hold on, and we'll see how Scripture backs this up. But for now, selah.

One short warning. This graph is not perfect. Don't try to pick it apart, apply it in every situation, etc. See it as a simplified explanation of God's dealing with Israel in their relationship to the Great Commission.

For Further Thought

For individual and small group study:

Think through another exercise on looking at world events as God does. Quickly list two or three current events that have fostered negative reports about Christians or simply about "Christian" America. Then imagine yourself as a member of an unreached people group.

How does that news affect your image of the true God?

How could God use even those events to reach these people groups with the truth about Himself?

List ideas new to you from this chapter's discussion.

List questions raised in this segment of study.

List any individuals from other cultures who may be

getting their understanding of Christianity through your life.

Find passages of judgment in the Scriptures and see where there was disobedience in the context.

Explain the blindness graph as if to a child.

Reference the phrase "I will hide my face" and see if there is any connection between this and blindness.

Pray for God's reputation in South America.

Chapter 6

The Importance Of An Obedient Heart

You've flown west out of Lima on a numbing seventeen hour flight to Jakarta. Then you met the squirrely little prop plane which took you to Irian Jaya. And now you're in a Missionary Aviation Fellowship helicopter clattering over some of the most treacherous, dense jungle on earth.

The island used to be called New Guinea; now this western half is Irian Jaya, one of the territories belonging to Islamic-dominated, animistic Indonesia.

Mike Meeuwse, the pilot, is singing, "Once I was blind, but now I see . . ." He looks like Tom Selleck.

"So, tell me the story of this Nipsan tribe," you prompt.

Mike constantly peers around at the gray-blue thunderheads to the north and south as you approach a bank of cliffs rising out of the lowland jungle. The chopper cab is sticky, humid under the relentless sun. "Some of the most unpredictable weather in the world is right around here," he muses. He points to several thousand-foot waterfalls cascading from the cliffs as the helicopter banks into a canyon, heading for the primitive highland village of Nipsan—fifteen years ago the site of a grisly massacre of believers, and today site of a remarkable feast of celebration.

"Garrett Khyte is the Netherlands Reformed Congregation missionary who felt led to reach that unreached group back in the early '70s. Like many of the other 250 or so people groups in Irian, the Nipsan were head-hunting cannibals. Not exactly the kind of place to raise your kids." But that's what he did. Went in with his wife and family and started a school with the blessing of the Indonesian government. The Nipsan spoke a Yali dialect, so Garrett asked in, as teachers and helpers, several Pass Valley evangelists who spoke a similar Yali.

"Then it started," his voice became more serious.

"Some of the young men at the school started acting like big shots around the village chiefs. There's a whole cluster of villages in the tribe. We just call the whole group after the main village, Nipsan. And then the Nipsan chiefs started noticing how the Pass Valley evangelists and their families cooked their pigs. Seems in Nipsan, you've got to whisper something in the pig's ear before you kill it. The Pass Valley Christians didn't whisper anything; and they singed the hair off before they cooked it. So the chiefs became convinced that the Christians were releasing evil pig spirits into the villages."

Mike pauses as the helicopter swings between ridges, following a rushing, brown river up into the highlands under the tropical blaze of the sun.

"Once when Garrett and his family had been flown out, the head chief ordered each village to invite one of the Pass Valley missionaries for dinner. As they arrived, the villagers attacked the wives and children back at the main camp. Fourteen men, women and babies were killed and eaten. For the sake of the Gospel."

You bank over a light ridge and see ahead a cleared valley with hundreds of scurrying figures, blurred by wafting smoke. You're suddenly concerned about this feast you've been invited to.

"A few believers escaped. And the head Pass Valley missionary, fellow named Saboonwarek, happened to be out of the valley. They got word to Garrett, so he had some of our MAF planes fly over regularly just to keep contact. The villages immediately had a catastrophic earthquake that altered the streams and completely ruined all their gardens. Reports came out of neighboring tribes that the Nipsan were actually starving as a people. So Garrett started dropping sweet potatoes out of the planes. But each time when they'd fly over the next day, he'd see the sweet potatoes chopped up and thrown in the river. That's how hateful they were."

Mike begins the procedure for landing in the clearing as, for the first time, you peer down and see the Stone Aged Nipsan people group.

"One day, about four years after the massacre, Garret told the pilot to land. Then, this gutsy missionary steps out with an ax. A crowd of the Nipsan cannibals come rushing up. Garrett offers one of the men the ax as a gift. The guy slowly reaches out and takes it. Can you imagine?"

"And then—?" you say, as the chopper settles on the ground, swishing dust and the smoke from the feast fires in all directions.

"Garret nods. The man with the ax smiles . . . which means they'll accept him again. So he moves his family back in, takes Saboonwarek with him as the main missionary, and for the next dozen years sees the wildest harvest imaginable. Hundreds of Nipsan turned to Christ in wave after wave of conversion . . . . an entire people movement to Christ." Mike gestures through the window as the engine cuts and the blades throb to a stop. Wild, greasy figures, reminiscent of National Geographic photos of painted cannibals, rush like hungry children to your window. Mike smiles: "They're your brothers and sisters. They'll be seated beside you at the marriage feast of the Lamb."

"And today's feast, incidentally," he adds, unbuckling his seatbelt, "is marking a new round of baptisms. Saboonwarek, the Pass Valley tribe missionary whose fourteen fellow-workers' heads were taken by these people, is doing the baptizing. And the first one to get baptized tomorrow? The head chief. The guy who ordered the massacre. He's now your brother."

Later, during the strange celebration of the feast, you marvel at the power of the gospel, God's plan to reach every people group with the blessing of redemption. You know that if the fourteen Pass Valley martyrs had been Western missionaries, there would be books about them, films, monuments. But here in the remote, primitive highlands of central Irian Jaya, the saga is simply one "incidental" scene in the story of God's plan for the Nipsan.

Here the terror and love of obeying God's command to reach every people seem raw, real. You think of Garrett Khyte handing the ax to that tribesman. You think of Saboonwarek returning to Nipsan, baptizing the chief. You think of the Pass Valley men and their wives and children risking everything, giving their lives so the Nipsan could join them around the throne of the Lamb.

Then you think of Christians back home; people praying as to whether or not to put new carpeting into the sanctuary; the medium size church down the road borrowing from the missions fund to buy a new organ; new buildings; new programs; but little that deals with reaching out to the nations.

Here in Pass Valley, the no-holds-barred obedience to bottom line responsibility is unnerving. It makes you wonder if American Christians are even aware of the reality of the spiritual world war raging over the great unchanging purpose of God. Back home, the battle seems so far away, so unrelated to God's global cause. Obedience to God's big-picture mandate is so abstract.

You're beginning to worry: Are we blind to the realities of God's global drama?

Biblical Revelation

Scripture is clear that God uses blindness. Turn to Isaiah, Chapter 6:1. "In the year that King Uzziah died, I saw the Lord seated on a throne, high and exalted, and the train of his robe filled the temple."

Isaiah says, "I saw the Lord." With respect to the graph in the last chapter, does this reflect high insight or low insight? High insight. Very high insight, close to "mega-insight"!

"I saw the Lord . . . holy, holy, holy, is the Lord God Almighty." Look at the next verse, verse 4. "At the sound of their voices the doorposts and thresholds shook and the temple was filled with a sweet aroma."

Objection! That is not what the Word of God says. Yet, think about it. If you were to envision the Lord standing there, wouldn't it be nice to have a sweet aroma filling the room? Roses and flowers from all over the earth just permeating the air, raising one to a zenith of excitement, of joy. That's not what happened to Isaiah. Rather, the room was filled with smoke.

Why smoke? What does it do? It burns your eyes so that you close them, and it obscures your vision. Isaiah's insight was diminished.

Look at verse 5. "Praise the Lord, for I caught a glimpse of the living God." Objection! That's not what it says. Actually, Isaiah panicked. "Woe is me, for I am a man of unclean lips, and I live among a people of unclean lips." He knew his insight was off the graph, yet he also knew he was sinful and he was doomed and destined for judgment. This is why it says in the Old Testament, "No man can see God and live." Too much insight and we're dead, because of our sin.

Notice that God supernaturally takes care of Isaiah's sin. What does God do?

Isaiah continues; "Then I heard the voice of the Lord saying, 'Whom shall I send? And who will go for us?'"

Now, does the text give any hint as to what that "go" is in reference to? No. Therefore it probably was in reference to something that should have already been well known. What could that be? Of course, going out to all the nations, the bottom line of the covenant. So, to whom was God directing this passage? Israel. There is nothing in the text showing that it was directed soley to Isaiah. God is asking, who, in Israel, His Great Commission people, would go to the nations.

How many respond out of an entire nation? One. Isaiah's humbled voice gulps, "Here am I. Send me!" Not much of a response for a whole nation. In fact, a terrible, disobedient response.

Look at what God says: "Go and tell this people." Now, if God had said, "Go and tell these peoples," of whom would He be speaking? Right, He would be telling Isaiah to go and speak to the nations.

But He says, "Go and tell this people," which could very easily mean He's referring to Israel. Why would

God want Isaiah to go back and talk to Israel? Because of their tremendously disobedient response.

So, He's saying, "Go back and tell Israel these words." What do you think He'd tell them in response to their disobedience?

He continues in verse 9 and 10: "Be ever hearing, but never under-standing; be ever seeing, but never perceiving. Make the heart of this people calloused; make their ears dull and close their eyes."

Through Isaiah, He's telling Israel that because of their tremendous disobedience, he's going to have to give them ears that cannot hear—hear what? God's Word—insight. Eyes that cannot see—see what? More insight. A heart that will be calloused to God's Word.

Why are they not going to understand God's Word? Because of God's knowledge of their future disobedience. Their reluctance to go to the nations is prompting God to keep them less accountable. He's lowering their insight by not making them keen to understand God's Word.

Then you read in verse 10, the word "otherwise." Otherwise what? Otherwise—had you said you would go to the nations and help fulfill the bottom line of the covenant—"they might see with their eyes, hear with their ears, understand with their hearts, and turn and be healed."

Had they chosen to obey the bottom line of the covenant, God would have given them all of the insight in the world (eyes that can see and ears that can hear), because they would not have had to be judged.

Because of Israel's refusal as a nation to go to the people of the world, God blinds them. If He hadn't, their guilt line would have quickly crossed His tolerance level. He would then have had to judge them by destroying them, which would have ruined His reputation. And His promise to fulfill the bottom line of the covenant would be in jeopardy.

Briefly, let's look at another passage, Isaiah 29:9-12: "Be stunned and amazed, blind yourselves and be sightless. Be drunk but not from wine; stagger, but not from beer. The Lord has brought over you a deep sleep. He has sealed your eyes (the prophets), He has covered your heads" (the seers)." These passages suggest low insight.

Who is the one doing the blinding? The Lord. Who is blinded? "For you"...who is the "you?" Israel. Are they choosing to be obedient or disobedient? Disobedient. "For you (who are being disobedient) this whole vision is nothing but words sealed in a scroll" (verse 11).

If it's only words sealed in a scroll, they can't understand it. It's "Greek" to them (actually Hebrew!) . . . keeping them less accountable so God doesn't have to judge them and ruin His reputation.

God is dealing with an entire nation here. But for illustration's sake, let's say He applied this blindness principle in your hometown church. You're listening to a sermon that leaves you excited, on the edge of your seat. You've been drinking in every word, and the hour has flown by in two seconds. As the last hymn is sung, you're digesting the truths of the sermon; you want to put it into action. You're walking out of church two inches off the carpet. As you're being jostled through the doorway, you overhear someone say, "That was the most boring sermon I have ever heard in my entire life. I didn't think it would ever end."

Now, without playing Spiritual Life Committee chairman, do you think that person plans to obey what he heard? Probably not. Now think of the possibility of God's merciful blindness: Because of God's knowledge of that person's future disobedience, God may have blinded him to prevent his understanding that sermon.

Remember, God doesn't throw pearls before swine. To those Israelites who chose to be obedient, God gave insight. For those who chose to be disobedient, the message is like a bunch of meaningless words on a scroll that's not even opened.

Let's look at another passage, in Isaiah 42.

Speaking of Israel, it says, "Hear, you deaf, look, you blind, and see. Who is blind but my servant and deaf like the messenger I send? Who is blind like the one committed to me, blind like the servant of the Lord? You have seen many things, but have paid no attention. Your ears are open but you hear nothing" (verses 18-20). Clearly, this is high disobedience.

Look at the next verse. You can almost insert a "therefore." (Therefore) "It pleased the Lord for the sake of His righteousness to make His law great and glorious."

One aspect of God's law being great and glorious is that it is difficult for many to understand. Many people read the Bible and get absolutely nothing out of it. Why would God allow it to be difficult to understand?

Well, think of the reverse. If God's law weren't difficult to understand, many who read it would be held accountable. And if they were choosing to be disobedient, what could the long-term outcome be for them? Judgement.

So with God making the law great and glorious-difficult to understand—upon whom must we be 100% absolutely dependent in order to understand it? God and His Holy Spirit.

And how do you think the Holy Spirit is going to determine whether He's going to give us insight into His Word? That's right. Based on His knowledge of our future obedience or disobedience.

That is why you should not say to God, "Lord, show me Your will for my life and then I'll determine whether or not I'll follow it." God will not show it to you, because He must first know of your 100% commitment to obedience.

Dozens of other passages deal clearly with this topic, such as: "You have neither heard nor understood; from of old your ear has not been open. Well do I know how treacherous you are; you were called a rebel from birth. For my own name's sake" (or another way of saying that, "for my own reputation") "I delay my wrath" (Isaiah 48:8-12).

How did God delay His wrath? By bringing a spiritual blindness on Israel, keeping them less accountable. What would happen if He judged them in His wrath? His reputation would be ruined, and then all the peoples of the earth would not consider His worthiness to be praised. So for the sake of His praise among the Gentile nations, God withholds His wrath by bringing about blindness.

Eyes That Do Not See

Did Jesus acknowledge these principles of blindness?

In Matthew 13, Jesus teaches the parable of the sower. The disciples then pull Him aside and say, "Why do you speak to the people in parables?" (Matthew 13:10). Good question; why didn't Jesus just very clearly spell out His teachings?

Jesus says, "The knowledge of the secrets of the kingdom of heaven have been given to you, but not to them" (verse

11). Who's the "you"? The disciples. Did they usually choose obedience or disobedience? Obedience.

"But not to them." Who's the "them"? The Jews. Did they usually choose obedience or disobedience? Disobedience.

The "knowledge of the secrets of the kingdom"—high insight—has been given to you (who choose obedience), but not to them (who choose disobedience). Then Jesus goes on. "Whoever has will be given more, and he will have in abundance." It's typical of Jesus, He never fills in the blanks. "Lord, whoever has 'what' will be given more of 'what'?"

Whoever has a heart for obedience will be given more insight, and he will have insight in abundance.

Notice the next part of the verse, "but whoever does not have (what?), even what he has will be taken away from him." Whoever does not have a heart for obedience, even the insight he has will be taken away from him.

Have you ever known a strong believer who walks with the Lord, and then suddenly falls into sin? If he refuses to repent and clings to that sin, what begins to happen to his heart?

His heart is hardened more and more. Whoever does not have a heart for obedience, even what insight he has will be taken away from him. Based on His knowledge of our future obedience or disobedience, God acts, and He can withdraw the power of His spirit from us, which will harden our hearts. This explains what took place with the Pharaoh. He hardened his heart in Exodus 5:2, and from then on God hardened it even further.

Sharpen your vision: Begin to look at even familiar verses with an eye to note the blindness-disobedience, insight-obedience pattern. For instance, notice John 14-21. "Whoever has my commands and obeys them, he is the one who loves me. He who loves me will be loved by my Father, and I too will love him and will show myself to him." Put the first part and the last part together. Whoever obeys Me . . . I will give him much insight. A direct link between obedience and insight. Of the one to whom much has been given, much is required.

Blindness Today?

Do you think God is still blinding today? Is it a Jewish phenomenon only, or could it be Christian as well?

Are there whole congregations in your town who are, in all sincerity, engaged in every social activity you can imagine to foster fellowship, but who are not really concerned about the heart of the Gospel? If so, is God blinding them?

Don't get into a judgmental, holier-than-thou stance on this, but imagine what would happen if God took away the blindness affecting many of our churches. What if He showed every church in the Body of Christ everywhere a vision of His great purpose to reach the nations so clearly that they could not disagree with it? He might then have to judge them, because perhaps many of them would not be obedient to the vision.

Think of it. What would happen if God judged all the churches around the world according to their strict obedience to the Great Commission? Zap/ Zap/ Zap! The earth would be swallowing up little and big congregations of God's people worldwide.

And God's very reputation would be ruined. Think what all the non-Christians (along with the Hindus, Muslims, Buddhists, etc.) considering Jehovah as their God would say. They'd probably respond to God's judgment with "Thank you, I think I'll stick with my own philosophy if that's the way God treats His people!"

Does God judge disobedient believers eventually? Yes, at the judgment seat of Christ (see 2 Corinthians 5:10, for example). But for now, out of His mercy for His children as well as for non-Christians, God blinds them.

Yet, before we end, let's think through some other reasons why God might be in the blindness business.

Could your parents be blinded? If they are, why didn't God zap them back when they might have been more accountable? Well, had He done that, who wouldn't have come along? You!

Because God knows of future generations that will choose to be obedient, he holds off judgment through blindness.

What might also happen to your parents two or ten years down the road? They might repent and get in on the greatest task on the face of the earth. That could be another reason.

But let's ask an even more personal question. Were you blinded to this material before you read this book?

If so, why is God giving you insight now? Right. God knows of your future obedience. It is not by accident that this book is in your hands and that you are understanding this material.

Let's end this chapter by saying this: Once we've finished our study together, you're going to love this book, and you're going to hate this book. You're going to love it because now you have greater insight. You're going to hate this study because now you have a tremendous amount of responsibility.

You can't go back. Your life can't ever be the same. God has given you increased insight and you need to be obedient in your response. You need to act on your new insight, getting more and more involved in the thematic backbone of God's Word. If not, months or years down the road this book could be collecting dust as you hastily go about the business of "Christianity," having forgotten—been blinded to—the depth of God's heart for all nations.

Selah.

For Further Thought

For individual and small group study:

List other ideas new to you from this chapter's discussion.

List questions raised in this segment of study.

Scan the chapters, noting especially meaningful

references and mark these in your personal study Bible.

Evaluate your life and see if there are any attitudes of disobedience which may be keeping you from insight.

See if this statement is true in your life, "I'll go anywhere, do anything, or say anything for God's kingdom." If not, what could the ramifications be?

List reasons why God might judge America. How could that judgement come?

Pray for a missionary movement among the Nipsan tribe.

Chapter 7

Seeing How It All Fits Together

Finally, an Ephesians 3:20 experience; they messed up your flight to China and you flew standby—first class! Settling into the noticeably larger seat, you give your drink order as you are handed a complimentary copy of USA Today. You adjust the seat backward and begin to browse through the newspaper. It's great to read U.S. news again. You begin to drink in the fresh news from around the world, after coming out of the heart of Nipson territory.

You finally drift into the editorial page. As you scan the page, you come across the headline "WHO COULD HAVE GUESSED IT?" You chuckle to yourself without even starting the article. "Well, of course God could have; one day, more of the media will realize who He is."

As you begin to breeze through the article, you realize the writer is responding to recent events in Eastern Europe. "It took ten years for Poland to gain its independence. Germany gained it in ten months, Yugoslavia in ten weeks, and Bulgaria in ten days."

Your mind begins to reflect on the missions conference held at your church two months ago. East Germany— what did they say about it? "Our mission agency had an offer for one million dollars to pass out tracts on the East German border. We turned it down because 30 million had already been passed since the wall came down. That is three tracts for every man, woman and child in East Germany . . . . We have also had an offer from an Eastern European country that has given us a building to start a Bible school for its people. They are coming to us. We have also totally depleted our stockpile of Bibles, which in a matter of days was dispersed among the peoples throughout this Eastern country. Romania already has a Romanian Missionary Alliance, and Far East Broadcasting Company (FEBC) is hoping to set up a Christian radio station within the country."

"Boy," you think to yourself, "God is really doing something in Eastern Europe."

"Here's your Diet Sprite with a twist of lime," the flight attendant says, interrupting your thoughts. Sipping on your drink, you continue to scan this article, now commenting about the Soviet Union. Glasnost...taking the world by surprise.

"Oh, yes," you begin to think to yourself. "Didn't my college roommate tell me that even the Soviet Union is inviting some of the major student groups to begin work on its college campuses? The FEBC has reported receiving

4,000 letters from the Soviet Union in one week! And aren't they now printing Bibles in the Soviet Union, though before they wouldn't let them in? And aren't the Christians in the Soviet Union starting their own missionary sending agencies?   Wow, God is really doing something there."

With no rhyme or reason, your mind all of a sudden begins to think about China and Tienanmen Square. "Didn't one of the missionaries tell me that more intellectuals have come to know Christ since Tienanmen Square than in the past ten years in China? Didn't another say that more Chinese are open to the Gospel since that event than in the previous years that he had been there?"

"Wait a second," you think to yourself. "Of course God could have guessed it, but did God plan it?"

Your mind begins to race. Could God be arranging these major events in history to bring about His purposes here on the earth? Is He using Iraq's invasion of Kuwait for His purposes?   Are all these major events linked to each other? Are they happening because of God's promise to Abraham?

Linking the Major Events Toward His Goal

Did you ever wonder why God said to Abraham, "Abe, I'm going to give you all of this land, but you can't have it right now. You are going to have to go away for 400 years of captivity before you can have it?"

The answer is found in Genesis 34. Here, Dinah had been violated by Shechem of the Hivite tribe. In his love for her, he wanted to marry her. He asked permission from her father—he was willing to pay any bride's price. Notice her family response: "Because their sister Dinah had been defiled, Jacob's sons replied deceitfully as they spoke to Shechem and his father Hamor. They said to them, 'We can't do such a thing; we can't give our sister to a man who is not circumcised. That would be a disgrace to us. We will give our consent to you on one condition only: that you become like us by circumcising all your males. Then we will give you our daughters and take your daughters for ourselves. We will settle among you and become one people with you. But if you will not agree to be circumcised, we'll take our sister and go.'"

Notice the latter part of the response. What could have happened to the descendants of Abraham and the Shechemites? They could have become "one people"! What would that have meant to the distinct tribe of Abraham? It would have been lost—scattered through co-mingling with nation after nation. Why didn't God just allow Abraham to stay in that land and grow and multiply?

Abraham's descendants were living among peoples with a similar cultural background. Because they were not that distinct, it was quite possible for the Israelites to intermarry with other people groups and lose their ethnicity.

If any of these had been the result, the promise God made to Abraham could not be fulfilled, because it was made to Abraham and His descendants. If their ethnicity had been lost, the covenant would have been lost. God needed a work to keep them as a distinct ethnic group. But notice one other thing. Jacob's sons replied "deceitfully." They weren't telling the truth. Why? What happened? You've read the rest of the story—they killed the Shechemites. What did that do to their reputation, and their God's reputation? "Uhmmm, boy, don't trust those Israelites—or their God! They're not to be messed with."

With this type of a reputation, what nation would want to follow the God of Israel? We've seen this before through Moses! Notice what else Jacob said. "Then Jacob said to Simeon and Levi, 'You have brought trouble on me by making me a stench to the Canaanites and Perizzites, the people living in this land. We are few in number, and if they join forces against me and attack me, I and my household will be destroyed.' But they replied, 'Should he have treated our sister like a prostitute?'" (Gen. 34:30,31). They could have been destroyed by any other nation avenging the Schechemite incident. So in order to erase a bad reputation over time and save the ethnicity of His people, God sent them into 400 years of Egyptian captivity.

God specifically wanted to make them a great nation in Egypt (Genesis 46:3). Why there?

There are many reasons. The first deals with the broad cultural differences between the Egyptians and the Hebrews. The Egyptians were polytheistic rulers, and the Hebrews were monotheistic slaves. This itself made the Hebrew people reject the Egyptian culture, and thus the Hebrews would never intermarry with the Egyptians on a large scale. Also, the Egyptians protected the Hebrew people politically. Under Egyptian protection, they were allowed to grow and multiply greatly. (Exodus 1:7). As a result, the Hebrew people were not destroyed in the Promised Land by any group going on a rampage, possibly trying to revenge the Schecemite incident.

The 400 years that transpired from the time of Joseph's entering Egypt and the Exodus also allowed the sin of the Amorites to reach its "fullness." What does fullness mean with respect to our graph on blindness? That's right. Judgment. It took 400 years of the Amorite's sin to become so great that God had to act out of hatred for sin, bringing about His judgment.

Another reason God put Israel under Egyptian captivity was that He wanted to use the Exodus to establish His reputation throughout all the earth. Remember the plagues? the Red Sea? All of these miraculous events allowed God's reputation to be established. In Exodus 5:1-2, we find out that God's reputation had not been established prior to these events.

The Promised Land

As God took the Hebrews out of Egypt, He placed them back in the Promised Land. We already know that the Promised Land was a very strategic piece of property, but there is more beyond that.

As the sin of the Amorites had reached its fullness, God had the Hebrew people retake the Promised Land by destroying all the other nations. That seems to show that A is greater than B, but it's not. If you look at it through an A=B set of lenses, God's destruction of all those nations came about because their guilt line had crossed God's tolerance level and He was bringing about judgment as he would have with any nation. It just so happened that God was using the Hebrew people to bring about that judgment.

This answers the age old question, "How could a loving God destroy so many people in the Old Testament?" It wasn't done as an A>B vengeful act; rather it was an A = B holy act, destroying the tremendous wickedness of the nations in the Promised Land.

Many of the laws God gave the Hebrews in the Promised Land were also to be a testimony to the visiting nations.

Imagine the reaction of the nations when Israel planted no crops for an entire year, the seventh year. "What, you're not planting any crops this year? You must be crazy."

"Our God says He will provide for us, and we are trusting in Him."

As that Gentile would come back a year later, what would he find? Still enough grain with which to trade and to eat. When he came back the next year with new crops coming in, he would again see that there was still enough grain. Through this, whose reputation would get established? Of course, God's. He was establishing His reputation through the laws He was giving His people in the Promised Land.

He also gave other specific commands which may seem to denote A is greater than B. Look at Deuteronomy 7:3: "Do not intermarry with them. Do not give your daughters to their sons or take their daughters for your sons." Do not intermarry with them—that surely makes it sound as if God's love for the Hebrews is greater. Was it just to keep them distinct as a people? What was the rationale? Is there any kind of any A=B perspective here?

The key is found in the next verse, verse 4-"They will turn your sons away from following me to serve other gods . . . ." If the Hebrew men turned to follow other gods of the nations, what would they have to offer the nations? Nothing. They could not offer them the God of Israel, and they would thus be unable to enjoy the top line blessings or fulfill bottom line responsibilities.

God knew that if the Hebrews—without the power of the Holy Spirit—intermarried with other nations, they would follow those nations' gods rather than bring those nations to follow Him, the God of Israel. If they followed the other nations' gods, they would never be able to offer them the good news of the Gospel, the top line blessings. If they couldn't offer them the top-line blessing, surely the bottom line would never be fulfilled. As a result, God said they were not to intermarry for their own sake, as well as the sake of the nations.

The Kingdom Divided

Later, the nation of Israel had three kings in the Promised Land who, good or bad, held the people together as one nation: Saul, David and Solomon. God replaced Saul, a bad king, with David. God replaced good King David with his son Solomon. Solomon started out as a good king, but strayed. And whom did God replace him with? Two kings; God divided the kingdom.

Now, why didn't God do with Solomon as He had done with Saul? God could have replaced Solomon with his son. Instead, He divided up the kingdom. There must have been some reason beyond personal disobedience such as seen in Saul, that caused God to completely split the kingdom of His Chosen People.

Remembering that every major event in the Story

of the Bible has top line and bottom line ramifications, let's think through God's rationale for dividing the nation.

1 Kings 11 tells us that Solomon had "seven hundred wives of royal birth and three hundred concubines . . . As Solomon grew old, his wives turned his heart after other gods, and his heart was not fully devoted to the Lord his God, as the heart of David his father had been. He followed Ashtoreth, the goddess of the Sidonians, and Molech, the detestable god of the Ammonites . . .

"On a hill east of Jerusalem, Solomon built a high place for Chemosh, the detestable god of Moab, and for Molech, the detestable god of the Ammonites. He did the same for all his foreign wives, who burned incense and offered sacrifices to their gods" (1 Kings 11:3-8).

Solomon had hundreds of wives of foreign descent— Ammonites, Hittites, the Pharaoh's daughter, and on and on. And they were all probably homesick!

If you've ever been overseas for more than a year, what's the greatest thing you can get from home? American hamburgers? No. Mail, right? There's nothing like hearing about what's happening in the homeland.

Solomon had a household full of foreign correspondents who regularly passed news on to their families, their friends, their own people groups. And how did they find out about what was happening at home? By listening for their homeland dialects down in the marketplace. By catching up on news from travelers and passing message packets to traders coming through Jerusalem, the world trade-route center.

What do you think these wives told the traders from their homelands? "Hey, go back and tell our people that Solomon is beginning to worship our gods. The God of Israel is passe'!"

As the traders would plod into or stride out of Jerusalem, what did they see that would authenticate the news? High on the mountain east of Jerusalem were temples to other gods. God's reputation was being destroyed. So what did God do?

He could have turned the nation over to Solomon's son Rehoboam. But read through 1 Kings 12 to realize that God's reputation would only have suffered more degradation among the nations, because Rehoboam was a terrible king. Had he taken over everything his father owned, he really would have destroyed God's reputation.

Disobedience that affects the Name of God, that threatens the fulfillment of the bottom line of God's promise to every people group, is always followed by judgment. Hence God divided the kingdom, another major event hinging on the Abrahamic Covenant.

Dispersion

Israel was special, but God's equal commitment was to spread His Name to all the nations.

Actually, at no time did God's love for Israel get in the way of His commitment to His own reputation and thus His glory among the nations. To God, A is not greater than B. He was willing to divide the kingdom, to allow His people eventually to go into captivity for the sake of His reputation among the earth's peoples.

Listen to God's heart:

"It is not for your sake, O house of Israel, that I am going to do these things, but for the sake of my holy name which you have profaned among the nations where you have gone. I will show the holiness of my great name . . . the name you have profaned among them. Then the nations will know that I am the Lord, declares the sovereign Lord, when I show myself holy through you before their eyes" (Ezekiel 36:22-23).

God wants to evangelize all the world, to fulfill His top line/bottom line purposes. His people are being disobedient. They are so wrapped up in themselves that they forget to be obedient to the bottom line and are even missing out on the top line!

So God says, "I the Lord am going to scatter you, all the Jews, like a whirlwind among the nations" (Zechariah 7:13-14).

In Ezekiel 5:12 we find that a third of them died from the plague, a third of them died from the sword, and the last third got dispersed to the nations as God's judgment struck this disobedient group. Notice the irony of the passage from Isaiah that begins this chapter. God uses the nations—the very people groups Israel is to be blessing—to carry out His judgment.

While in captivity, the third who were dispersed repented. And, naturally, they then became a witness to the nations. Remember the testimonies of Daniel, Shadrach, Meshach and Abednego? God, in His sovereignty, will reach every people with the blessing of redemption, and since the Israelites wouldn't go to the nations, He sent them to the nations through the Babylonian and Assyrian captivities. He brought down two birds with one stone—their judgment and world evangelization!

It was God's "involuntary go-mechanism".

The effects were incredible; even the great King Nebuchadnezzar repented and proclaimed that everyone in his Babylonian kingdom was to follow and worship the God of the Jews.

Imagine: You're a people conquered by the great Nebuchadnezzar, and you read his order to worship a non-Babylonian God. For years you've heard the rumors about Nebuchadnezzar being reduced to the state of a mindless beast by this God—he was crazy for seven years. Now he's in his right mind, and he's issuing orders to worship that God of the Jews. Perhaps you'll follow orders. First, you need to find a local Jew and ask about this God—who is He? How do we worship Him? What are the basic beliefs?

. . . There will be people, Egyptians, Babylonians, etc., who acknowledge Him. Even if God has to use the disobedience of His people.

Homecoming

After seventy years of captivity, God orders His people back to rebuild the walls of Jerusalem: "I will bring health and healing to it (Jerusalem); I will heal my people and will let them enjoy abundant peace and security. I will bring back Judah and Israel from captivity and will rebuild them as they were before. I will cleanse them from all the sin they have committed against me and will forgive all their sins of rebellion against me" (Jeremiah 33:6-8).

That sounds like which part of the covenant—top line or bottom line? Top line. Since we know that with every top line blessing comes a bottom line responsibility, let's look at the next verse to see if the bottom line is there as well. "Then this city will bring me renown, joy, praise and honor before all nations on the earth . . ." (Jeremiah 33:9).

But even this remnant had trouble remembering their bottom line responsibilities as God's people. They again began hoarding God's blessings, refusing to pass them on. And since God blesses us to be a blessing cross-culturally, He began withholding Israel's blessings.

For example, as Israel scrimped on maintaining the Temple, a monument to the Name of God among all peoples, God withheld His blessings in ways that might seem faintly familiar today:

"Is it a time for you yourselves to be living in your paneled houses, while this house (of God) remains a ruin? . . . Give careful thought to your ways. You have planted much, but have harvested little. You eat, but never have enough. You drink, but never have your fill. You put on clothes, but are not warm. You earn wages, only to put them in a purse with holes in it. . . .

"You expected much, but see, it turned out to be little. What you brought home, I blew away. Why? declares the Lord Almighty. Because of my house, which remains a ruin, while each of you is busy with his own house" (Haggai 1:3-9).

As His remnant in the homeland repented, however, God again promised "From this day on I will bless you" (Haggai 1:19).

For Such a Time as This
Some of His people, though, never journeyed back

to the Promised Land, after the time of the captivity. After seventy years in Babylon/Medo-Persia, the Jews probably had their own schools set up. They had developed kosher food distribution systems; they had their own little forms of government. So they stayed. Did God use this?

The Book of Esther dramatizes the circumstances of those Hebrews who stayed in the lands of their captivity. Remember the basic story? Esther becomes queen of the Medo-Persian empire at exactly the right time to intercede in behalf of her Hebrew people.

If you have an A>B perspective, what was God doing as Queen Esther saved her people? He was simply protecting them from their enemies. But if you have an A = B perspective, several events of this wonderful story take on new significance—such as the gala ending: "In every province and in every city, wherever the edict of the king went, there was joy and gladness among the Jews, with feasting and celebrating. And many people of other nationalities became Jews because the fear of the Jews had seized them" (Esther 8:16-17).

Notice the area as listed in Esther 1:1: Every province, every city in the kingdom, which stretched from India to Ethiopia (Esther 1:1)! Individuals from all sorts of people groups in the Medo-Persian empire converted to Judaism. And in all probability there were many more who did not actually become Jews but who did decide to fear the God of Israel.

These "God-fearing Gentiles" passed that attitude on

from generation to generation. It was that event, through Esther, that set the stage for the Apostle Paul's evangelism to spread like wild-fire. Notice the term "God-fearing" Gentiles many times in the Scriptures (Acts 10:22, 13:26, 13:48, 17:12, 17:17).

So God used even Israel's disobedience and dispersion to fulfill the bottom line of the covenant. He said, "I will display my glory among the nations, and all the nations will see the punishment I inflict and the hand I lay upon them. From that day forward the house of Israel will know that I am the Lord their God. And the nations will know that the people of Israel went into exile for their sin, because they were unfaithful to me" (Ezekiel 39:21-23). God upheld His name among the nations.

A equals B. Do you see how every major event of Hebrew history in Scripture hinges on God's desire to fulfill His promise to Abraham and to reach both Jews and Gentiles? And those events shape a story with a single theme—a theme that gives us a clear sense of God's historic purpose, a theme stating a clear priority for our lives—bring God maximum glory by winning representatives from every tongue, tribe and nation!

For Further Thought
For Individual and group study:
List ideas new to you from this chapter's discussion.
List questions raised in this segment of study.
Scan the chapter, noting especially meaningful references

and marking these in your personal study.

List the major events covered in this chapter and from memory show how they relate to the Abrahamic Covenant.

As if you were preparing an open-book quiz for a class, write out five key questions on the material in this chapter. Then be sure you could answer them from memory!

Read the headlines of today's news and see if God is behind them.

Pray that God will raise up laborers quickly to fulfill His promise to Abraham.

Chapter 8

Understanding Jesus' Ministry

You're still spinning around the world on a trip that unnerves you. You're tired. This is your last stop. But you know it's a big world; and there are thousands of remaining unreached people groups you haven't even seen or known of.

So as you're in a mufflerless Jeep, barreling along the main highway skirting the foothills of the Himalayas, you try not to think about how many lost there are among the millions and millions of individuals in the People's Republic of China (PRC), alone.

The area is red-earthed and rocky, with bucolic views of valleys around every other corner as your official government guide squeals the Jeep along the last curvy stretch of paved highway, before you enter Naxiland in the Lijiang Valley in northwestern Yunan Province, in an area which has long been a hub of trade between Yunan and Tibet.

You've heard the remarkable statistic that there are

about 50 million believers in China right now. But you know most of those Christians are ensconced in the Han Chinese majority culture and they are not necessarily targeting the minority people groups within their borders.

Here in the southwestern corner of China, Yunan Province is home to twenty four distinct ethnic groups—most of whom won't be reached through typical, near-neighbor evangelism.

One of these twenty four is the Naxi (Naw'-shee).

You hang on as the Jeep hurtles through the cool, dry air on to a dirt and gravel road; and you review your unofficial notes cribbed from various China-watching groups back home:

Naxi—

Population: 240,000

Language: Similar to Tibetan. There is no written language, yet they once used a pictograph system for religious writings. Although they stubbornly cling to their ethnic traditions, many   Naxi now also speak Mandarin, the language of the majority Han Chinese.

Social structure: The Naxi people live in compact communities. Due to the influence of matriarchal social traditions, Naxi women   occupy the important roles in Naxi agriculture and horse-breeding. Living in large households ruled by the grandmother, Naxi women handle business affairs while the men play a domestic role, caring for the children and tending the garden.

A Naxi couple lives with a woman's family. She may have more than one husband, or she may share her sister's husband or husbands in a sort of group marriage. Marriage relationships are very informal: A young woman takes a man as a partner for several months, or years, or a few days. There is little concept of close relationship between father and child.

The official PRC line is, of course, that the Chinese people are one. They are simply called "The People." Actually, you see as you drive by road-construction sites and sporadic rustic houses, that the various people groups are definitely distinct—even in their dress. You begin to see more Naxi women along the roadside.

They wear traditional costumes of gray homespun, pleated skirts and capes which are dark blue above and white below, with a row across the back of seven tassled disks that glint in the high altitude, bright sunlight. The elements of this "firmament cape" represent the heavens. The blue symbolizes the night sky, the white is for daytime and the seven disks represent stars.

This quaint reminder of the Naxi link to nature is sullied as your Jeep roars into the outskirts of a small town and you glance at your notes on Naxi religion.

The Naxi worship nature gods in a mixture of Tibetan Lamanism and the ancient Bon religion, Buddhism, Chinese Taoism and spiritism. Their many gods and demons are placated and manipulated with magic and elaborate rituals involving blood sacrifices. Naxi shamans invite the gods or demons to possess them, and while in a trance they foretell the future and answer questions. Most of the gods are portrayed as fierce and terrible as they trample on animals or humans. Among the most fearsome gods is Yama, the god of death. His partner, Tsamundi, a goddess, is often portrayed as holding a skull-bowl full of blood. The Naxi are lifelong captives of fear.

You pull into a market area in the little town where several caped Naxi, tossing trayfuls of large, purple beans in the air, are winnowing the husks and singing together. In its simple exotica, the town isn't much of a reminder that you're entering a region held in bondage for thousands of years by the satanic god of death, Yama.

As the noise of the Jeep finally dies and you step down on Naxi ground, the thought of being one of the two or three known Naxi Christians among this quarter-million people group makes you shiver.

Isaiah 49:25 is, as it has been throughout your journey through the remote hinterlands of China, your consolation: "The prey of the tyrant (Yama) will be rescued."

You again pray in God's will that Satan's age-old domination over this people group will be broken, and you "beseech the Lord of the harvest to send out laborers into His harvest" (Luke 10:2), to bring foreign or Han Chinese Christians into Naxi land. What could the message of Jesus Christ do here? If He were on the earth, would an obscure place like the Lijiang Valley be His ministry base? Would He bother with ethnic minorities?

Jesus' Ministry to Ethnic Minorities

"When Jesus had heard that John had been put in prison, he returned to Galilee. Leaving Nazareth, he went and lived in Capernaum" (Matthew 4:12). Jesus based His ministry in Capernaum. Many Jews will say that Jesus was not the Messiah because He didn't headquarter His ministry in Jerusalem, the heart of Judaism. This is said with what kind of a perspective? You guessed it, A>B.

Some of the populace of the area spoke Latin, some in Decapolis spoke Greek, and in Capernaum most citizens spoke Hebrew. There was a distinctive mixture of Jewish and Gentile influences. Why did Jesus choose Capernaum rather than Jerusalem?

Matthew writes, "Jesus went through Galilee, teaching in their synagogues, preaching the good news of the kingdom, and healing every disease and sickness among the people. News about him spread all over Syria" (Mt.4:23-24). Was Syria a Jewish or Gentile area? Does Scripture say: "And the people brought to him all who were ill with various disease . . . And He healed the Jews and He sent the Gentiles home."? Obviously not. He healed "them," Jew and Gentile alike. And as they skipped and praised their way home, what do you think those Gentiles were talking about? This Jesus, this man who has the power to heal.

Why base His ministry in Capernaum? Because Jesus could have immediate contact with a whole spectrum of people groups. A equals B. So "large crowds from Galilee, the Decapolis, Jerusalem, Judea and the region across the Jordan followed him" (Matthew 4:25).   Not only that, but He also knew that Jews south in Jerusalem had enough motivation to move north and check out a possible Messiah, whereas Gentiles from Syria probably wouldn't have had enough motivation to take the long journey south to see a miracle worker.

There are plenty of simple passages in the New Testament describing Jesus' heart for all humanity. And there are many excellent commentaries on the Gospels' references to the Gentiles—any peoples that are non-Jewish.   So rather than studying these familiar passages, let's take a quick look at some of those New Testament passages that seem to suggest A>B—that Jesus did not come to minister to the Gentiles but to the Jews only.

For example, in Matthew 10, as He sends out the twelve disciples, He says, "Do not go among the Gentiles or enter any town of the Samaritans. Go rather to the lost sheep of Israel. As you go, preach the message, 'The kingdom of God is near'" (Matthew 10:5-7).

So much for the premise of our study together, right? If He were a whole-covenant Messiah, both top and bottom line, how could He possibly order them to "not go among the Gentiles"?

Let's fast-forward for a moment to the events of Acts 11.   Jesus has lived His life on this earth, risen from the dead, told the disciples to reach all peoples.   Now, after much time has passed, the "apostles and the brothers throughout Judea heard that the Gentiles also had received the word of God" (Acts 11:1).

But notice verse 20. They probably criticize Peter: "You went into the house of uncircumcised men and ate with them! Peter, you're our leader—how could you do this? We're going to have to start the impeachment proceedings." The disciples obviously weren't too happy.

Yet, once Peter reviewed the events of the conversion of Cornelius, the disciples "had no further objections and praised God, saying, 'So, then, God has even granted the Gentiles repentance unto life'" (Acts 11:18). As if it were something totally brand new.

Skip back to Matthew 10. If, at that later point, the disciples were still so squeamish and reticent to share their faith with Gentiles, how much more did they have that same perspective here at the beginning of the ministry of Jesus?

Can you imagine the disciples swimming across the Jordon and telling the Gentiles, "Hey, you Gentiles, guess what. God loves you and has a wonderful plan for your life." The Gentiles would look at each other and then jump up with excitement, exclaiming, "God loves us? That's terrific. Can we hug you?"

Of course the disciples, being firmly entrenched in an A=B theology, would lovingly reply.

"Oh well, at least come into our homes and get warmed by the fire. You must be cold, being you're so wet."

"No, we're not allowed into Gentile homes, it's against

our religion."

"Well, can we feed you? You must be hungry," they'd reply in trying to help those who had brought them such "good news."

"No," the disciples would retort. "We brought our own Kosher lunchs..."

Really, would it have been good news at that point? No.

So, it's as if Jesus basically said, "Look, gentlemen, you've got such an A>B perspective that you'll ruin any attempt to reach the Gentiles. Just go to the Jews for now and try to get this message straight. Later I'll send you to the Gentiles."

He's very clear about this "later" idea: "On my account you will be brought before governors and kings as witnesses to them and to the Gentiles" (Matthew 10:18). He seems to be telling them He'll send them to the Gentiles once they get the message down pat—the theme of God's blessing of redemption.

Notice in Luke 10:1-16 that Jesus later sends out the seventy-two, or   it could also be that Jesus sent out the seventy.   Whereas Jesus had sent out the twelve and instructed them not to go to the Gentiles, now he sends out the seventy and simply says go to everyone.

Now, those numbers, twelve and seventy, could be symbolic—twelve can represent the twelve tribes while Seventy can represent the nations. Regardless, this later commissioning makes it obvious that the earlier injunction to go only to the Jews was a temporary top line mandate. When He sent out the seventy, he gave the bottom line parallel mandate.

The Canaanite Woman

Let's think through the classic passage some use to suggest that Jesus wanted no dealings with anyone but Jews.   Read through Matthew 15:21-28:

A Canaanite woman from that vicinity came to him, crying out, "Lord, Son of David, have mercy on me! My daughter is suffering terribly from demon-possession." Jesus did not answer a word.

So his disciples came to him and urged him, "Send her away, for she keeps crying out after us."

He answered, "I was sent only to the lost sheep of Israel." The woman came and knelt before him. "Lord,

help me!" she said. He replied, "It is not right to take
the children's bread and toss it to their dogs." "Yes,
Lord," she said, "but even the dogs eat the crumbs that
fall from their master's table."

Then Jesus answered, "Woman, you have great
faith! Your request is granted." And her daughter was
healed from that very hour.

Now, how do we align this passage with the rest
of the Bible's top line bottom line, A equals B theology?
Very simply. Get a pair of scissors, cut the passage
out, and all of the Scripture will be harmoniously.

A equals B. No problem.

Seriously, let's analyze this unusual story. Let's look
at it in its context. Turn to the beginning of Matthew
15. Here Jesus begins to speak about what is clean and
what is unclean—the outside of the cup versus the inside—
that what is on the inside of the heart makes a man
clean or unclean. In other words, it doesn't matter whether
you're a Jew or a Gentile on the outside, what matters
is what's in your heart. He was giving them an A equal
B lesson! It's very clear.

But His disciples have what kind of a perspective?
A > B.

Notice (Mt. 15:21) that Jesus then leaves that Jewish
area and purposely withdraws to the region of Tyre and
Sidon—a Gentile area. Why does He do that? You guessed
it; He wants to run into Gentiles. Once they arrive, however,
a Gentile woman confronts Jesus and He remains silent.

Why?

Perhaps Jesus does not answer a word to the woman because He wants to test His disciples' understanding of His recent lesson. Have they learned their lesson? Obviously not: "Send her away," they say, "for she keeps crying out after us, Lord," as if saying, "it's about time you gave us a chance to speak up. Thanks for not saying a word; Lord, we'd really like to enforce this idea that your love for the Jews is far greater than for all the nations, those Gentile dogs. Let's just send her on her way."

So Jesus, in effect, said, "Look, there goes your A>B perspective again. Okay, is that the game you want to play? For the next thirty seconds I'll live it out the way you want it to be lived out." So He tells the woman, "I'm sorry, but I was sent only to the lost sheep of Israel."

Notice her response: "Lord, help me," she says.

He replies, "It's not right to take the children's bread and toss it to the dogs." Notice that Jesus actually calls the Gentiles dogs. He surely hadn't read Dale Carnegie's book on how to "win friends and influence people" by this time. Was using that discriminatory slang a healthy thing to do in Gentile Tyre? Probably not. He is obviously stressing some point.

And think through what He is saying: "It's not right to take the children's bread and toss it to the dogs." The term "children" represents what people? The Jews. "Bread" represents what? The blessing. It's not right to take Israel's blessing and toss it to the dogs, the Gentiles.

Is that true or false? False. It goes in direct opposition to the entire Old Testament's emphasis on top line and bottom line theology. Jesus here purposely misquotes the Abrahamic covenant! If Jesus is not speaking satirically, He is revising the Abrahamic covenant on the spot! But this He can not do without perjuring the Godhead, since Genesis 22:16 and Hebrews 6:13-18 reveal that God had bound Himself by an unchanging oath to fulfill both of the requirements of that sacred covenant.

Why would Jesus misquote such a basic teaching? Why does Jesus call the Gentiles dogs? Why does He say, "I was sent only to the lost sheep of Israel"? Perhaps because He is trying to teach His disciples something: to play the game of the disciples, acting out the A>B philosophy and demonstrating how far it could go. Somehow—maybe through the twinkle of His eye—Jesus non-verbally communicates to that woman, "Woman, hang in there. I'm trying to give my disciples an illustration of a lesson I just taught." Jesus keeps the woman coming back, coming back. Then (the Greek text hints) that at this point he turns and says, "Woman, you have great faith." Her daughter is healed.

It may be at this point in the role-playing exercise that Peter turns to James and says, "We've been had; He meant to heal her the whole time".

After Jesus went from Tyre to Sidon, He came back to the other side of the Sea of Galilee (Gentile area) and fed the 4,000. Earlier, He had fed the 5,000 Jews. When He comes to the feeding of the mainly Gentile crowd of 4,000, He says to the disciples, "Get them some food." Their response? "Lord, there's no way you can feed these people. How can we find food in this remote place?" Remote place? They were in Gentile territory. They were very uncomfortable. Now, they had just seen Jesus feed 5,000 men with their women and children. All He was asking them to do was to feed 4,000 men with their families, and they're basically saying, "It can't be done."

Why can't it be done? Because they figured that God would never feed Gentiles miraculously. But Jesus, being a whole-covenant Messiah, feeds the 5,000 Jews—top line—and then the 4,000 Gentiles—bottom line. He is a whole-covenant Messiah, fulfilling the whole law.

These major events are still revolving around the Abrahamic covenant. And this promise remains foundational, as is even demonstrated in the book of Acts.

In Acts 1:8 Jesus says, "You shall receive power when the Holy Spirit has come upon you, and you shall be my witnesses in Jerusalem and Judea and Samaria and the remotest parts of the earth." But the early disciples apparently misunderstand Jesus' words.

They think He had said, "...you shall be my witnesses either in Jerusalem or Judea or Samaria or the remotest parts of the earth"—as if there were a choice. And the choicest place to concentrate their witness is, in their estimation, where the church started—in Jerusalem.

Empowered by the Spirit, the disciples begin their ministry, appropriately enough, among an international Jerusalem crowd which was made up of "God-fearing Jews from every nation under heaven" (Acts 2:5). They miraculously speak in different languages of all the nations of the earth, showing how tongues initially had a direct relationship to world evangelization.

Peter addresses the crowd, thousands are saved, and the believers begin to grow in the apostles' teachings, in fellowship, in the breaking of bread and prayer.

Peter later speaks to the Sanhedrin (see Acts 3:24-26) and quotes Genesis 12:3: "It is you who are the sons of the prophets, and of the covenant which God made with your fathers, saying to Abraham, 'And in your seed all the families of the earth shall be blessed.'" Notice that he doesn't quote Genesis 12:1-2, which refers to the top line of the covenant. He knows that those trained in the Word of God already know well the fact that God wants to bless them.

He also knows they have an A>B mindset. So Peter reminds these onlookers and leaders of the bottom line A = B strategy: "When God raised up His servant (Jesus), He sent him first to bless you by turning each of you from your wicked ways" (3:26). That word "first," suggesting the top line, forces Peter's listeners to consider the next recipients of blessing—the Gentile peoples.

In Acts chapters 1 through 7, we find that the gospel was spreading like wildfire—but only within the city limits of Jerusalem. So what did God do? He brought about a tremendous persecution: "On that day a great persecution broke out against the church at Jerusalem, and all except the apostles were scattered throughout Judea and Samaria" (Acts 8:1). Sound familiar? Jerusalem, Judea, Samaria?

What happened as they were forced to scatter? "Those who had been scattered preached the word wherever they went" (Acts 8:4). God, in His sovereignty, allowed persecution so the gospel would get outside of Jerusalem—a vital step in the outworking of His unchanging purpose.

Get realistic about this. Did those Jews who were scattered own homes? Did they have investments and obligations in Jerusalem? Had their children been in good schools? Did they have jobs? Had they been perhaps comfortable and secure where they were? Why would God totally uproot them out of all of that? Because God is just as concerned with reaching the nations as He is with providing comfort and security for believers.

Remember that Jesus did not say Jerusalem or Judea or Samaria. His disciples were to be impacting all these areas from Jerusalem to the ends of the earth.

Up until this point in the book of Acts, if you look at Peter's ministry in Jerusalem (as seen in Acts 1-9,) what rating would you give him on a scale of one to ten? Seven? Ten?

God probably gave him a rating of about two. Let's look at the events of Acts 10 to see why.

Criticism About Cornelius

In Acts 10:9-16, Peter has a vision and is told to "rise up, kill, and eat." But Peter says, "Surely, Lord, I've never eaten anything unclean." The voice comes back to him, "Do not call anything impure that God has made clean" (10:15).

The scenario recurred three times. Why? To show Peter that the Gentiles are not unclean and that they needed to be reached with the Gospel (Acts 10:17ff). Notice how surprised Peter seems at his new insight: "I now realize how true it is that God does not show favoritism but accepts men from every nation who fear him and do what is right" (Acts 10:34-35). And notice the dumbfounded reaction of the Jewish believers with Peter: "The circumcised believers who had come with Peter were astonished that the gift of the Holy Spirit had been poured out even on the Gentiles" (Acts 10:45).

So, obviously Peter had been missing the point of his own preaching when earlier he had announced, "You are heirs of the prophets and of the covenant God made with your father. He said to Abraham, 'Through your offspring all peoples on earth will be blessed'" (Acts 3:25). Peter had apparently known that bottom line responsibility was part of the big picture of what God was doing. But he failed to make that responsibility practical. He had refused to act on it.

Selah.

Up until this point, Luke has been focusing on the disciples in Jerusalem. But in Acts Chapters 11-13, God has him in transition from solely the disciples and their Jerusalem ministry to the ministry of Paul and Barnabas. Then from chapter 13 on, God looks in depth at the ministry of Paul and Barnabas . . . focusing in on the bottom the covenant.

In Acts 15, Paul and Barnabas, missionaries to the Gentiles, meet with the church leadership in Jerusalem to decide what to do with all these Gentile believers.

It is obvious that God is operating on an A = B basis. James confirms the validity of the signs and wonders among the Gentiles by referring to Amos 9:11-12: "I will restore David's fallen tent . . . so that they may possess the remnant of Edom and all the nations that bear my name," declares the Lord.

The Jerusalem council decided that they would not trouble Gentile converts, but these new believers were to abstain from food sacrificed to animals and from sexual immorality (Acts 15:20).

Paul probably walked away saying, "Well, I lost a few battles but I basically won the war! I've got them realizing that we can reach out to the Gentiles freely and not make them become Jews."

From that point throughout Acts Chapters 16-20, there is no mention of Peter and the other disciples. Luke draws our attention to Paul and Barnabas in their bottom line outreach to the Gentiles. Try looking at the Book of Acts from an A = B perspective; you will begin to find that Luke focuses on the twelve disciples' disobedience, their reluctance to take the Gospel outside of Jerusalem. The disciples never seem to catch what Jesus said: "You shall be my witnesses both in Jerusalem and Judea and in Samaria and the remotest parts of the earth."

The Apostle Paul himself backs up this complaint about the twelve disciples' limited vision, as he later writes about that conference in Jerusalem. Notice his choice of words. He says, "Fourteen years later I went up again to Jerusalem . . . and set before them the Gospel that I preached among the Gentiles. But I did this privately to those who seemed to be leaders for fear that I was running the race or had run my race in vain." Those who seemed to be leaders! He's writing about Peter, James and John!

". . . As for those who seem to be important (Peter, James and John), whatever they were made no difference to me . . . Those reputed to be pillars gave Barnabas and me a right hand of fellowship when they recognized the grace given to me." Paul then records the council's delegation of missionaries to people groups: "—that we two should go to the Gentiles (two to 99% of the world's population) and that they (the twelve) should go to the Jews (12 to 1% of the world's population)" (Galatians 2:1-10).

These were absurd odds (suggested by those that seemed to be important) and a grossly unfair way to distribute the task; but that is exactly what was decided. Unfortunately, the disciples seemed not to fully realize their bottom line responsibility.

Later, post-biblical records indicate that many of the disciples did eventually catch the vision. Thomas possibly took the Gospel to India, Peter was hung upside-down on a cross in Latin Rome, and the other disciples dispersed to various places.

But it seems that the true message of the Book of Acts is not so much the obedience of the disciples to go out, but their reluctance to bless all the families of the earth. God had to use one who was persecuting Him to take the Gospel out of Jerusalem into Judea, and Samaria and to the remotest parts of the earth.

How have we done since then? Are we who seem to be leaders in the church just as shortsighted these days about following the simple mandate of Scripture to bless the peoples of the world?

Selah.

For Further Thought

For individual and group study:

Scan the chapter, noting especially meaningful references and marking these in your personal study Bible.

Determine a time to read completely through the book of Acts in one sitting. Consciously watch for the varying attitudes of A>B, A=B or possibly A<B!

List the past three major events in your own life. Ask yourself the question, "Was there any bottom line involvement there?"

Think through the next three significant events in your life. How will the bottom line be involved?

Spend five minutes in prayer for the Naxi unreached people of Yunnan Province in China.

Chapter 9

It's Been 4,000 Years;
How Are We Doing?

We have seen major events in the Story of the Bible hinging on God's desire to reach all the nations. God's promise to Abraham is foundational in the Word . . . even for today. Now let's get completely practical. If God has commissioned us to reach every distinct ethnic group on the face of the earth, how are we doing?

If a profit-oriented, multi-national corporation were given this challenge of reaching every distinct ethnic group with a sales offer, they'd have tremendous plans, goals and projections; they'd know where there was progress; they'd know where they were going in five years, in ten years, and so on.

Unfortunately, we as the Body of Christ have faltered in our planning, in our objectives, in tracking God's progress in this global project. We don't know where we're going. So it's time to assess where we are with the gospel, how we're doing and what our goals are to reach the nations.

The Picture Is Encouraging!

First, let's highlight part of a passage we've looked at earlier in our study: "When God made his promise to Abraham . . . He swore by himself, saying, 'I will surely bless you and give you many descendants . . .' because God wanted to make the unchanging nature of his purpose very clear to the heirs of what was promised, he confirmed it with an oath. God did this, so that, by two unchangeable things in which it is impossible for God to lie, we who have fled to take hold of the hope offered to us may be greatly encouraged" (Heb.13-18).

One of the objectives of our study of God's big picture is that you be greatly encouraged. God is going to finish this task. He is going to reach the nations, and you can be a significant part of that process. Perhaps you're catching through this study, an awareness that your life can be riveted with purpose and drive in a cause that is eternally significant.

Now, focus on the little phrase in Hebrews 6:17— "the unchanging nature of his purpose." If the ceiling were to blow off the building where you now sit reading so diligently, if the heavens were to open up wide and you were to see God and say, "Lord, what is it that's on your heart right now?"—based on His Word, we know that His response would be something like this: "I love you and want to bless you. And I want you to turn around and be a blessing to the nations, because I want every group of people on the face of this earth to know

My love." What's on His heart is unchanging.

You're blessed to be a blessing. He meant it when He said it at the time of Abraham. He meant it in the time of David. He meant it at the time of Ezekiel. He meant it at the time of Jesus. He meant it in Count Zinzendorf's time with the Moravians. And He means it now. It's His unchanging purpose, and He wants to make it very, very clear . . . to you.

Blessing all the world's people groups with salvation is the sum of the unchanging nature of God's purpose. We are co-workers with God in that endeavor.

Since this is His unchanging nature, how are we doing?

Record of the Unreached Peoples

World population has fluctuated from seventy distinct ethnic groups after the Tower of Babel, to 60,000 people groups at the time of Christ, down to approximately 24,000 distinct ethnic groups today. About 12,000 of these ethnic groups have been reached; they have a church movement within their culture that is capable of evangelizing its own people group.

Yet that means there are another 12,000 people groups who have not had their first chance to say "yes" or "no" to Jesus' love for them; 2.4 billion people who have no one in their culture who speaks their language, who could tell them about the good news of our Lord . . . . one out of every two people on the face of the earth.

Study through the following chart of the world's

proportions of believers, nominal Christians, and non-Christians who live in a culture where they can find out about the gospel. Then notice the non-Christians in unreached people groups who do not have an honest chance to say "yes" or "no" to Jesus Christ.

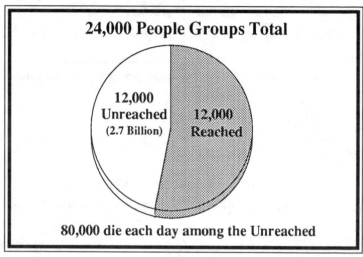

24,000 People Groups Total

12,000 Unreached (2.7 Billion)

12,000 Reached

80,000 die each day among the Unreached

Think about it: Right now, half the world's population doesn't have a chance to say "yes" or "no" to the blessing of salvation in Christ. May that never remain a cold statistic in our minds. But may it break our hearts, knowing that every day nearly 80,000 individuals in unreached people groups perish without God and without hope (that's 55 people a minute or roughly one person every second).

God's purpose is to see that all those 12,000 groups of people have a church. About 4,000 distinct Muslim people groups make up the largest cultural bloc of the unreached. Han Chinese people groups form another large segment of people without a viable church. Hindu, Buddhist and tribal people groups also are major cultural blocs without a Gospel witness.

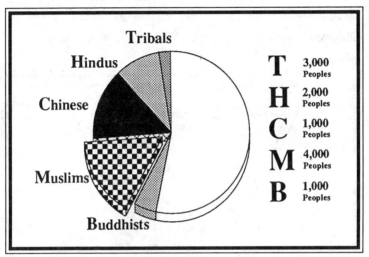

There's an easy way to remember them. Think of your thumb; "THUMB." "T" stands for Tribals, "H" is for the Hindus, "U" (turned sideways!) is for the Chinese, "M" is for the Muslims, and "B" is for the Buddhists. All are in desperate need of having someone reach out to them.

Resources for the Task: Personnel

Half the world's individuals have a church within their cultures and can learn about the Lord, and half the world does not have a church. If you were God, where would you send your best laborers, to the reached half of the world's population or to the unreached half?

It only makes sense that sending the best laborers to the unreached half is what the Lord, the Head of the Body of Christ, would do. So what is the Body doing? Look carefully through the following "Great Imbalance Diagram" until it hits you: We're not doing well at all, yet.

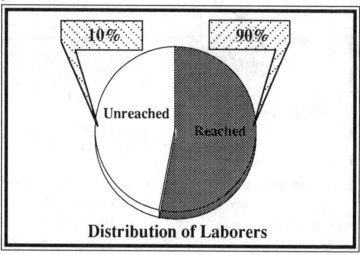

Distribution of Laborers

So nearly 90% of all our foreign missionaries go to the reached people groups, the half of the world where there already is a church established. Now, there's nothing wrong with that. Because where the church has been planted, it grows unbelievably, and these fledgling churches need encouragement and workers. Missionaries to reached fields are viable ministries.

But, we've got to face up to the fact that only 10% of our foreign missionary force is going to the totally unreached half of the world, where roughly one person every second dies without ever hearing about Christ.

That's foreign missionaries. If you were to look at the number of full-time Christian workers' ratio, you'd find for every worker going to unreached peoples, 171 go to a culture where there already is an established church. That's 99.9%.

Let's be blunt with ourselves: Is this imbalance of laborers God's will? Is this the way God planned it? Or is it perhaps evidence of the disobedience of the Bride of Christ in not responding to the commission God has given us to do?

Resources for the Task: Finances

Gird yourself for a few more uncomfortable factors before we get to the encouraging news of what believers are doing to establish a church in every people group on the globe.

On the average, for every dollar that gets put into the offering plate in the United States, 96% goes right back into the American Christian culture. Out of the remaining 4% for the Great Commission task, 3 1/2 cents go to the world's people groups where there's already a church. Less than one penny goes to reach the unreached peoples of the world where there is no church. This is the product of an American A>B theology.

The Need for Resources

If the Body of Christ were to tackle the task of the

Great Commission in earnest, what would be needed in terms of personnel and finances? Not to mention prayer power!

How many new missionaries are needed to effectively penetrate the remaining 12,000 unreached people groups? Many missiologists say a team of eight well-trained missionaries could effectively be used by God to plant a viable church in an unreached group. That is, 96,000 new missionaries are necessary, since current missionaries are deployed in other areas where, again, their ministries are critical to growing churches. Adding another 4,000 new missionaries to the total would take care of the natural attrition of retirement within the evangelical missionary force.

What finances are necessary for the task? Support for these 100,000 individual missionaries and provision for their ministry projects would require, experts suggest, an additional $1.5 billion dollars annually!

That's the discouraging news of world evangelization. The discomforting news of what is happening in this world.

The Resources Available

The good news is this: We can do it. We have the resources.

Remember Deuteronomy 32, where God orders the inheritance of the nations in direct proportion to the number of the sons of Israel? God didn't allow the nations to grow any faster than He let Israel grow, because if revival ever broke out, He would be able to realistically reach every nation through the Chosen People. Has He maintained that ratio today?

Believe it! For every single unreached people group in the world today, there are 416 evangelical churches. For every one of these unreached people groups, there are 41,600 evangelical believers!

God will accomplish His purpose. The gates of hell that lock in the unreached peoples of the world can't stand against His church. At the end of time Christ will be exalted with the song "...and with your blood you purchased men for God from every tribe and language and people and nation" (Revelation 5:9). So it's only a matter of when and through whom.

Of the 70 million evangelicals in America, 17.5 million are aged 18-35. The 100,000 new missionaries needed are only half of 1% of these young people available just in the USA.

American evangelicals have $850 billion of disposable annual income. About one-fifth of 1% of that income—$1.5 billion—could support the needed 12,000 church-planting teams. That's one nickel of every free dollar we have.

But this isn't a job for just American believers. With 430 million other believers worldwide, obviously the resources are available. We can establish a church movement in every unreached people group, and then help those new believers to evangelize their own people group.

We can do it if we will.

The Timing Is Everything

Remember when we talked briefly about Matthew 24:14: "and this Gospel of the kingdom shall be preached throughout the whole world as a testimony to all nations and then the end will come"? Again, regardless of your theological position on the timing of the events of the last days, it's obvious that the accomplishment of God's unchanging purpose on earth is linked to the end.

Think through the implications of the following passages:

> Matthew 28:18-20—"disciple all nations". . . to the end of the end of the age"
>
> Acts 1:6-8 "witnesses...to the ends of the earth" (v.8) "restore the Kingdom to Israel" (v.6)
>
> Romans 11:25-26—"until the full number of the Gentiles has come in"—all Israel will be saved"
>
> Revelation 5:9—"[The Lamb] purchased men for God from every tribe and language and people and nation"—His breaking the seals of the scroll initiating a new era.

Let's look at another interesting passage, 2 Peter 3:2, where we're commanded to "look forward to the day of God and speed its coming"! How can we possibly speed the coming of the day of the Lord? Perhaps by reaching all nations, tongues, tribes and peoples so that His promise to Abraham can be fulfilled.

Humans are almost driven to insist that everything will go on as it has since the beginning of creation (2

Peter 3:4), but God reminds us that there is a definite time limit for what He is doing on the earth "until the coming of the salvation that is ready to be revealed in the last time" (1 Peter 1:5). God is waiting on something. What is it? To see the full number of all ethnic groups reached; and then He's going to come.

We can "speed the day"! Selah.

Take a big look at the history of God's people and their efforts to evangelize the world. From the time of Noah to now, what have we done?

The Jews, as we've seen, faltered in their world evangelization campaign. But God worked despite their disobedience.

Christ's disciples seemed to catch a glimpse of vision for the peoples of the world, but it was just a small, hesitant glimpse. Many believe that the twelve disciples never really caught the vision at all since they determined to remain in Jerusalem. It was Paul and Barnabas who owned that vision and first went on into Gentile territory.

After that came 300 years of persecution, and that persecution spread the Gospel throughout the Mediterranean. Then the emperor Constantine made Christianity the official religion. You would think it a good move, but it was actually a very destructive move, because now everyone could become a Christian. In fact, everyone virtually had to be a Christian; there was no cost in following Christ. There was little emphasis on spreading this bland state religion to the ends of the earth.

During the Dark Ages, it seems that the idea of the Great Commission wasn't even considered. There were small groups of believers, of course, with small ideas of reaching the world, but a movement as a whole never came about. During this reign of barbarism, naturally, God was accomplishing His determined will to spread the good news to all peoples through a series of migrations. As people groups moved, the believers among them began to spread the blessing of redemption in Christ. Even the forays of the Vikings and other "barbarians" into Christian lands, spurred on the spread of God's blessing. The misguided Crusades fueled some spread of the awareness of God's plan of redemption—but again, on the whole, believers seldom united with a sense of purpose in blessing the nations to the ends of the earth.

Even the era of the Reformation produced little vision for the world. Luther's and Calvin's Protestantism explored the theological aspects of personal salvation in Christ, but seemed to remain focused on the top line. There were a few groups that caught a sense of God's great global purpose—notably the Moravians—but they were few and scattered. There was no sense of a movement of God's people as a whole until the 1790's. Then an Englishman by the name of William Carey announced, "You know what? I'd like to go evangelize the heathen in India." His church elders responded to him: "Young man, when God wants to reach the heathen, He'll do it without your help and without ours."

Astounded, Carey wrote a little booklet about our obligation to evangelize the heathen throughout the world and then proceeded to practice what he preached. He headed for India and spawned a movement to evangelize the coastlands of the world's continents. The men and women of this movement were stalwart, no-holds-barred zealots who often set sail with their belongings in a casket because they knew they only had an average of two years to live in the disease-ridden areas. They felt the priority of evangelizing the world was far greater than saving their own lives. But, for various reasons, the first wave of modern mission interest began to die down.

Then in the 1860's Hudson Taylor fostered a second movement of reaching the unreached in the inland regions of the globe. He founded the China Inland Mission. Out of that came Sudan Interior Mission. Out of this movement also came Africa Inland Mission....and Regions Beyond Missionary Union, etc. Nearly 20,000 new laborers volunteered as missionaries during these years.

Still, championed by the amazing energy of the Student Volunteer movements in America, even this powerful second wave of preaching the unreached began to fizzle in the mid-twentieth century.

Women played a key role in both movements. Ruth Tucker and Walter Liefeld in Daughters of the Church felt the womens' role was the backbone of it all.

But we now find ourselves in the possibility of a third movement, a third wave or era in modern missions. Perhaps the final era.

Responding to Cameron Townsend and Donald McGavran's call in the second half of this century to go to the culturally isolated "hidden" or "unreached" peoples, many believers sense that this third wave is surging to the breaking point in this last decade before the year 2000. God is doing amazing things in our world. He's sending Navajo missionaries to the Mongolians, shaking up American finances for His worldwide cause, blasting open the Iron Curtain, raising a movement of excited disciples ready to go anywhere and do anything. He's harvesting more than 70,000 new believers every day. Eminent world watchers sense an upcoming burst of God's power in this final decade of the twentieth century, during these closing years of the second millennium.

Yet in light of the 4,000 or so years man has been here since the time of Noah, notice that in the past 200 years that God has poured out his Spirit in a new and unparalleled way. Why only now?

Opportunity for Harvest
The population growth of Planet Earth now is skyrocketing as never before. Ten billion people have lived on this planet, through all of history.

To have the first one billion people alive at the same time, took 9,830 years. To bring the population to two billion, took an additional 100 years. To bring the population to three billion, took an additional 30 years. To bring it to four billion took an additional 15 years, and to five billion took another 14 years. The next one billion will take eleven years.

What took 9,830 years to do is going to take only 11 years to do!

The population of this planet is exploding in exponential growth. By the year 2000, world population will reach about 6.26 billion. Often that population growth is seen as a cause for discouragement in reaching the world's unreached. Actually, it's an incredible time of opportunity for completing the Great Commission! If there was ever a time to be alive on this planet called Earth, it is today.

Since population growth is no surprise to God in His unchanging purpose, perhaps we simply need to sit down and realize that if we reached the world now, we'd be able to impact more people then has ever been possible.

These are exciting days as God is pouring out His Spirit and giving us fresh insights into His purpose for the world's peoples. Why us? Why now?

First, because He knows our possible future obedience. But second, the movement to reach every people with the Gospel is growing because, now, more than at any time in history, there are simply more people to bring into the Kingdom in a brief period of time!

God has now entrusted us with the technology, the transportation, the communications, the finances, and the power to finish the Great Commission. God has provided everything so that we can accomplish His task in a more concentrated time-frame than was ever previously possible. For example, just in the past few years it has become possible to codify whole languages into computerized translation programs to produce Bible translations and church-planting tools in a fraction of the time it required just twenty years ago. You can be anywhere on the globe in twenty four hours. We've got the tools. We can do it. We can evangelize the world.

We are living in the most exciting time in the history of the world, the unfolding of God's unchanging purpose. Christianity's largest denominations have dedicated this decade to world outreach. Many Christian leaders believe these final years of the twentieth century will witness the greatest spiritual harvest the world has ever seen.

Believers in various countries are "adopting" unreached peoples to target. For example, South American Christians are planning to send teams to 3,000 unreached groups. North American churches are targeting 6,000.

Christians worldwide are getting excited, realistic and specific about throwing themselves into the final era of God's unchanging purpose. And prayers are being lifted up that you are one of them. Selah.

For Further Thought
For individual and group study:
List other ideas new to you from this chapter's discussion.
List questions raised in this segment of study.

Scan the chapter, noting especially meaningful references and marking these in your personal study Bible.

Jot in a handy one-or-two-page summary the basic information in this chapter; then explain that information to at least two other believers this week.

Glance back over previous chapters to be reminded of the various people groups you've met in this DESTINATION 2000 study. Then get serious about praying for them for at least 15 minutes this week.

Contact the U.S. Center for World Missions (1605 Elizabeth St., Pasadena, CA 91104) and have them send you some information that you could share with your church regarding adopting a people group.

Pray that churches around the world would begin to think about adopting an unreached people group.

Chapter 10

It's Very, Very Do-Able

The Big IF

It's a fact: If the Body of Christ began to think strategically and would target resources to send one team to plant one church to each unreached people group, we could evangelize the world in our generation. Easily.

But of course the big word is "if," if the Body of Christ begins to think strategically, if it responds to the unchanging nature of the purpose of the Head. Frankly, it seems that many people in the Body of Christ are not thinking strategically. They actually have no clue as to what God is doing, that He has made clear His unchanging purpose from Genesis to Revelation to reach every people group in the world.

The consequences of this unclear vision of God's purpose are obvious. King Solomon stated that "where there is no vision, the people perish" or, more literally, "lose restraint" (Proverbs 29:18). People naturally lose focus, and have no reason to discipline themselves even in moral areas if there is no constraining task to tackle.

If the Great Commission were a mandate to reach 5 billion individual people with the Gospel, it would be obvious that God gave us not the Great Commission, but Mission Impossible.

Without a very clear, realistic vision, it's easy to think, "Lord, I haven't even reached my next-door neighbor yet. How could I ever reach more than 2 billion people? Lord, I think I'll just stay here and try to be a good Christian."

But when you realize God has commanded us to reach 12,000 distinct ethnic groups, all of a sudden the job is do-able. Perhaps you decide: Actually, my church could adopt one of those groups, and especially if we got together with nine other churches in our town, surely we could see a church movement planted in that group. Then those new believers could reach out to their own culture in more effective ways than a foreign missionary ever could.

The Great Commission is very, very do-able. It is within our reach if we begin to pray that God would open up the eyes of the church and allow us to think strategically about world evangelization.

Look What God Is Doing!

If you're in a dull little corner of Christendom, it is critical that you realize what God is doing these days around the globe. Here are a few highlights.

1,600 new churches are opening every week

worldwide!

28,000 become believers every day in China. Conservative estimates say there are 40-50 million Christians in that country.

20,000 become believers every day in Africa; that continent was 3% Christian in 1900 and is over 40% Christian today.

A total of 70,000 become Christians every day!

In 1900, Korea had no Protestant church; it was deemed impossible to penetrate. Today, Korea is 30% Christian, with 4,000 churches in Seoul alone.

In Indonesia, the percentage of Christians is so high the government won't print the statistic-- which is probably nearing 25% of the population.

After seventy years of oppression in the Soviet Union, Christians number about 100 million - 5 times the number in the Communist Party and 36% of the population.

God is creatively sending Chinese believers to reach Tibetans, Hondurans to reach Lap-landers and Mongolians.

Where the church has been planted, it's growing like wildfire. The good news is breaking loose worldwide:

More Muslims in Iran have come to Christ since 1980 than in the previous 1,000 years combined.

> In AD 100, there were 360 non-Christians per true believer. Today the ratio is seven to every believer.
>
> In AD 100 there were twelve unreached people groups per congregation of believers. Today there are 416 congregations for every unreached people group.

That's what God is doing. What are we doing?

That unchanging purpose places a greater priority on the mandate of the covenant than our own personal goals, dreams, desires and security. Remember Namaan's little Hebrew slave girl? She had goals. She had things she wanted to accomplish, but God allowed her to become a slave to a foreigner because of His love, His intense love for a Gentile (2 Kings 5:1-27).

Jonah had plans. He had legitimate fears. But God had a job beyond Jonah's plans and fears. It's as if God said, "I've got something better for you, Jonah. I want you to go to Nineveh, because I love the Ninevites" (Jonah 1-4).

God is willing to forfeit our ease to see His goals and purposes brought about. That's what the Lordship of Jesus Christ is all about. Jesus says in Luke 14 that we must be willing to give up ownership of all we possess if we are to be His disciples. The possessions aren't just material things. We possess goals, dreams, desires, careers, all sorts of intangible things. And we must be willing to lay these at the foot of the cross if we want to see

Him accomplish through us all that we can do.

Your Part in The Big Picture

Perhaps you're a young person striking out on a career. Or you're older, struggling with the quandaries of a career change. The questions are familiar to all of us. Some might ask, "God, what are you calling me to be? Do you want me to be a Christian housewife, and really do a good job at that?" Others might say, "Lord, am I to be intensively involved in discipleship and prayer? Is that where you want me?" Still others, "Lord, is my domain, my reservoir of life-giving water, supposed to be that of a Christian engineer? Am I simply to be a testimony to those at my office? I'd like to be a good Christian chemist. Or how about a lawyer? Maybe I'll teach Sunday School on the side for a ministry. Maybe I'll be a dentist, or a pastor, or a real estate agent. Lord, what do you want me to do?"

Somehow, we begin to get a bit self-centered about God's will for our lives. The prime question seems to be: "What is God's will for my life?"—as if A were far greater than B! Might it be a Christian dentist, might it be a children's worker? Am I to do this or to do that? And somehow we think that each possibility is basically unrelated to all the other roles of God's people. We think of our career as an isolated little lake way over here and God's will for another believer's career as a little lake way over there.

But we must begin to think of ourselves, not as isolated pools, but as contributing parts of the whole composite of God's will. Each of our lives can release its potential into the mighty river of God's ultimate plan to reach all nations.

If you are a Christian pastor, you're to be equipping men and women to have a vision for the glory of God, to disciple others to get involved in the Story of the Bible of reaching all the nations. If you are a Christian housewife, you're to train and raise up godly children who will be so sharp and so well versed in His Word that they can intercede for missions and even go cross-culturally to reach the nations.

If you are a chemist or a doctor or a lawyer, you're being blessed by God with financial blessings, among others, so that you can turn around and be a blessing to those who are more directly involved in reaching the nations. And you, yourself, can be involved in reaching the nations through prayer and through encouragement of other workers who go to the nations . . . even through reaching internationals in your area.

But you're not simply to be a dentist or real estate agent or sales rep off by yourself. You're to plug into God's big-picture plan to reach all the nations. Everything we do is to reach that zenith of seeing every people group reached and thus to bring a maximum amount of glory to God.

Blessed to Be Blessed?

Think about the emphases of our Christian culture in America. Why are we trying to heal marriages? So we can be happier, be more and more blessed? So we can say, "Oh, praise the Lord, we've got a good Christian marriage now"—and sit back, comfortable and secure?

No. We're to heal marriages so these people, united together in strong marriages, can become so strong and so secure that they say, "Look, I think we need to get involved in reaching out to the Asians here in our local community." Or, "Why don't we think about going and serving God over in the Middle East among the Muslims?"

Why are we trying to save our youth from crack and drugs and alcohol and sex? Do we want them to just say no so they'll have easy, nice lives? No, we want them to say no so they can grow up without being damaged, with a good self-image, so they can walk with God in holiness and purity. They'll then be the person God needs to stand in the gap, to work in the rigors of real discipleship so that our Lord's heart can be fulfilled in seeing all the nations reached.

If you have a vision to reach your neighborhood, your town or even all of America, rejoice! You're seeing God's heart for 5% of the world's population. But reach your Jerusalem and Judea, clothe the needy and feed the hungry, witness across the street and stand up for the unborn with an expanded vision of God's whole heart for the uttermost parts of the world, and get to know the rest of your God!

Minister within your own people group to bring your neighbors to Christ; equip them to join the cause of reaching every people group with the Gospel. Encourage the growing churches on established mission fields by training them to be missionary—sending churches. Directly or indirectly, be a part of God's historic purpose to add to the Body of Christ those "purchased with His blood from every tribe and tongue and people and nation."

What is God's historic purpose? To bless His people—including you as a believer—and directly or indirectly, through them, to offer to every people group on earth the blessings of salvation in Jesus Christ.

God has a job for you, and it has to do with the 12,000 unreached people groups of this planet. It is God's ultimate purpose for today's busy Christian.

The Countdown!

We're almost 4,000 years into God's promise to Abraham that all the people groups would be blessed with redemption, and the plan is intensifying. Hundreds of mission groups worldwide have seen AD 2000 as an arbitrary target date to finish the task of reaching each people group.

Since, as we've studied, Jesus simply said, "This Gospel of the Kingdom shall be preached in the whole world for a witness to all the people groups, and then the end shall come" (Matthew 24:14), you might feel uncomfortable about AD 2000 as a target date to see mission teams among each of the 12,000 unreached groups . . . as if the year 2000 is then some prediction of the return of Christ. Relax. The countdown of people groups to be reached by the year 2000 is simply an arresting way to suggest that we can complete the Great Commission within a few years—if we will. At a world-level conference in Edinburgh, Scotland, 70 mission groups from thirty-seven countries adopted the phrase "A Church for Every People By the Year 2000."

But if date-setting feels awkward, imagine that it's 2041 and we can reach all remaining groups within seven years. Would 2048 be a less threatening target date than 2000?

But why wait, when every day 80,000 unreached souls go to hell—one every time your heart beats (which is one of those uncomfortable Bible truths we don't like to think about)? If the lost weren't lost, why would God command us to disciple the nations at all? The Bible says these very real people—individual by individual—are without God and without hope (Ephesians 2:12). Study this distressing fact in the Word. Then ask yourself, "Why wait?"

We can establish a church for every people group by the year 2000. And you can be a part of this urgent, historic, big-picture priority.

Your Part in the Big Picture

It is time to pray and beseech God to raise up laborers

to go to the very ends of the earth. The verb Jesus used to "thrust laborers out" means to actually push them out even if it's against their own will. Its the same Greek verb (ekballo) used when Jesus cast the money changers out of the temple or when you cast a demon out of a person. Why such prayers? Probably because God knew how infatuated we would be with the top line. It is time that we do the job that will be the finale of 4,000 years.

Let's get radical and simply obey the Great Commission to reach every people group in the world. Now. Let's pray for it. Fast for it. Encourage our brothers and sisters to put their lives on the line. We have an unparalleled opportunity—a window that's wide open.

Many people are saying that in the year 2000 we should present Jesus a birthday gift—the gift of an evangelized world. And that's why many young people are giving up top-line-focused careers. Retired couples are giving up "the good life" and joining teams overseas. Thousands of young and older believers are giving up the BMW's and going for the big bucks; they're saying, "Lord, I want to be used strategically by you to see this world evangelized, and I'm going to work for it toward the year 2000."

The Catch

If the biblical mandate is so clear, if the big picture of what God is doing in our world is so exciting, if the

12,000 remaining groups can be reached within several years, if millions are dying without God and without hope, why isn't all Christendom buzzing with the news that we can finish the task?

Because there's a catch. There's a cost involved.

Obedience costs. Real discipleship costs. The price is giving up any small, local agendas that detract from God's global cause. The cost is to forsake our little lives. To give up claims of ownership and security. The requirement for ministries is to cooperate selflessly rather than needlessly duplicate efforts and compete for funds.

Obedience means shifting our focus to being a blessing instead of just being blessed—the vision problem Haggai pinpointed as the downfall of Israel.

The price of being a part of God's global purpose is losing your life for His sake.

Active participation in the big picture of God's plan is also dangerous. It's the danger of signing on in wartime as a soldier who doesn't entangle himself in the affairs of everyday life (2 Timothy 2:4). Battling the powers and world forces (Ephesians 6:12) that have bound these 12,000 groups for thousands of years means spiritual warfare; and warfare means casualties, body counts, blood, sweat and tears.

God's big purpose on this planet is not a game. It's not a health spa regimen. It's war. And war is never nice.

Maybe too many Christians have been led to believe that the true believer's life is supposed to be nice, respectable, predictable and smooth. Or maybe they actually have counted the cost of discipleship in God's big plan. Then they decided they're too weak for real battle and refuse to trust the Commander's strength.

But what about you? Is there any good reason you and your fellowship aren't taking seriously the mandate in God's historic purpose to disciple the nations? You could "adopt" a people group and see to it that the countdown number is lowered to 11,999!

A Neglected Challenge

Consider one very significant category of unreached people groups—the Muslims of the world.

Few American Christians know much about Islam. This ignorance keeps them from acting or having a significant role in seeing that churches become a reality in the heart of the Muslim world. God cannot lead where there is no knowledge. So open yourself a bit more to His leading— and learn about Islam.

The word "Islam," in it purest essence, means "submission to God." A Muslim (one who follows Islam) is one who submits to God. The very heart of the religion is that Muslims are trying to seek the face of God.

Today they represent 17 percent of the world's population—nearly one out of every five people on the face of the earth. They span the globe, but reside mainly in the Asian area. Only one quarter of the Muslim world is Arabic-speaking.

There are forty-four predominantly Muslim countries throughout the world. In these countries there has never been a church established; or the church is too small and inward to influence Muslims; or it has become extinct.

Some churches in these countries are basically indifferent to their Islamic neighbors' needs for Christ. One pastor in a predominantly Muslim country said, "Hell, it's the best place for them." There are such radical differences that most "historical Christians" in this man's area would prefer to see Muslims go to hell. Churches in largely Islamic countries are generally constituted almost entirely of people from non-Muslim backgrounds, with cultural patterns abhorrent to Muslims.

Though these statistics are alarming, the news gets even worse. Less than one percent of our total Protestant missionary force works among Muslims. This means that there are more missionaries to the state of Alaska than there are to the entire Muslim world. We simply have not made Muslims a priority. Our financial patterns are revealing: Less than one-tenth of every penny given to the church goes to the Muslim world.

What Muslims Believe

Muslims believe they must do five simple things to work their way to heaven.

First is their witness. They must confess that there is no God but Allah, and Muhammad is his prophet.

Second, a Muslim must pray five times a day. These

prayers are short, lasting an average of two minutes, and are said from memory. Muslims pray at approximately an hour before sunrise, 10:00 A.M., 1:00 P.M., 4:00 P.M., and about an hour after sunset.

Third, a Muslim needs to tithe his income. Muslims tithe one-fortieth of their income to help the poor. Many Muslims give their tithe directly to needy people on the street.

Ramadan is the fourth way to earn entrance into heaven. This is the fast. The Muslim fast is different from the Christian fast in that it lasts for one lunar month from sunrise to sunset. During this time of day, Muslims are not allowed to have anything pass down their throats. This way they again relate to the hungry of the world.

Fifth, a journey to Mecca, the birthplace of Islam, must be undertaken if one can afford it. This is a very holy pilgrimage for the Muslims, and they derive great satisfaction from it.

Some missiologists add a sixth requirement, the jihad, which literally means "exerting force for God." One's jihad might be accomplished through writing a book about Islam, trying to share one's faith with someone, or physically fighting for the cause of Islam. This is what Iranian leader Khomeini sustained for so many years against Iraq, a holy fight—a jihad for the cause of Islam.

In Islam, the only eternal security one has is dying in jihad. If death comes during jihad, one is guaranteed the keys to heaven. Now you can understand why there are individuals driving a truckload of dynamite into U.S. Marine barracks, blowing themselves and the Marines to smithereens. In doing so they are guaranteed their entrance into heaven.

In essence, Muslims will tell you that there is a good angel on one shoulder and a bad angel on the other. When you get to heaven, there will be a judgment day, and if your good works outweigh the bad works, you will probably go to a sort of purgatory and eventually make it to heaven. If the reverse is true, you will go to hell forever.

Some Islamic beliefs are similar to Christian beliefs. Muslims believe in one God, as well as good and bad angels. They also believe in many prophets. All Muslims believe in Adam and Eve, Moses, David, Abraham, and even Jesus, but their final prophet is Muhammad, who gave the ultimate revelation about Islam.

They believe in certain holy books—the Torah (the first five books of the Old Testament) and the Zabur (the Psalms) the Ingil (the New Testament—officially only the four Gospels) and their Quran.

The Quran is considered to summarize all the other books while adding more. Muslims believe that our Bible has been corrupted and cannot be trusted; thus they have no copies of it and do not feel that they need it, because "the Quran covers it all" and needs nothing added to it.

A Place to Belong

In reality, what keeps a Muslim a Muslim is 90 percent cultural and only 10 percent theological.

Muslims need to belong to an extended group of individuals in order to feel secure. They do not buy the Western idea of "be independent—be No. 1." Usually, the primary group to which they belong is their extended family. It is in that extended family that they find security and meaning and purpose.

In Muslim terminology, this belonging is "ummah."

Picture it. A missionary sits down and gives a Muslim the invitation to come to Christ. What is going through the Muslim's mind?

"You mean you want me to leave my extended family where all my security is—socially, financially, physically— and tell me all of that is wrong and they're going to hell? . . . Sure, tell me another one!"

Leaving his "ummah" is the hardest thing a Muslim faces. The theological differences between Christianity and Islam are tough, but Muslims can get over them. Theology is only 10 percent of the problem.

Complicating the issue even more is how Muslims view Christianity. Did you know that Muslims believe that we worship three Gods—God the father, God the son and God the mother? And that threesome came to be when God came down to earth, saw Mary, lusted after her, and had sex with her? No wonder they believe Christianity is simply "out to lunch."

This concept of an immoral religion is confirmed in Muslims' minds when they turn on the television and watch "Christian" programs. They assume that "Dallas" and "Dynasty" are Christian TV programs and that they exemplify Christianity.

The overall effect? In considering the claims of Christ, most Muslims start at a negative 15 rather than 0. They need to work their way out of these misconceptions before they can hear the good news of Christ.

Extending a Hand to Islam

Sound disheartening? Or simply challenging? There are those Christians who are excited about reaching Muslims for Christ, who believe that God is initiating a great work in the Islamic world. One such group of people is FRONTIERS.

FRONTIERS is looking to place 2,000 new missionaries on 200 new teams in the Islamic world by the year 2000. It is our goal to send teams to see churches become a reality.

FRONTIERS has five distinctives.

First, we work solely with Muslims. We do not work with Hindus, Buddhists, Chinese, or tribal groups. We are a bit like Kentucky Fried Chicken: We do one thing, and aspire to do it right!

Second, we send out teams as opposed to individuals, for we believe that the Bible encourages this model. (For more information on how our teams work, write to FRONTIERS, (P. O. Box 40159, Pasadena, CA. 91104) and ask for our brochure titled "Questions and Answers to

FRONTIERS" and "One in a Million.")

Third, each team goes to plant a church. We are not there only to do evangelism or discipleship—the end goal is an established church.

Fourth, we coach the teams on the field. Experienced missionaries travel frequently to visit the teams, passing along strategies and news of other teams, and helping team members catch a better understanding of what is going on in the world.

Last, we encourage diverse and creative approaches in pursuit of our unifying goal of seeing churches planted in the Muslim world. We realize that everyone will not fit the same mold, so we allow a wide variety of molds within FRONTIERS.

We do not require seminary or Bible school of our candidates. A much more pressing concern is that they have a working knowledge of the Scriptures and a vital, vibrant walk with God. Each team member must also be sent out by a home church.

We accept retired couples as missionaries. We are actively recruiting individuals to "retire" on the field with our teams. Often we find these older folks to be the glue which holds our teams together.

Every team is flexible. Each makes many of its own policy decisions about furlough, children's education, retirement, and finances. Team leaders decide where their team goes, and only they can approve or deny placement on their team.

As of the publication of this book, FRONTIERS has fifty-nine teams either on the field or preparing to go, with over 240 missionaries on Muslim soil. We have grown very quickly in a short amount of time, but we feel that is God's stamp of approval on us.

As you continue to grow in your world vision, we would make one request—please consider the Muslims. With only one missionary for every one million Muslims, we need people like you.

You may be saying to yourself, "Hey, wait a minute, you don't even know me." You're right. But we do know the God that lives inside of you . . . .

If you are interested, please fill out the "I'm Interested" form in the Appendix Section of this book.

For Further Thought
For group or individual study:

Explain how doable the Great Commission really is.

List the five unreached blocks of mankind.

Share some of these simple statistics with a friend.

Explain the basics of Islam in your Sunday School class.

Seek to find Muslims in your area and befriend them. Ask them to share with you what Islam means to them.

Read through the appendixes in the following pages. Choose five application steps from Appendix B and act on them.

Appendix A

If God has been tugging on your heart to get involved in the Muslim world, please consider joining FRONTIERS. Your first step would be to fill out the "I'm Interested" form on the following pages. There is no obligation in doing this, you are merely 'testing the waters'. We'd love to hear from you. Or call us at 1-800-GO2-THEM (462-8436).

Appendix B

This Appendix has a listing of all of the scriptures this author has found that deals with God's dealing with the nations, the bottom line. Highlight your Bible with these mission verses and see how they all relate to the Big Picture. Feel free to copy this section and pass it on to your friends.

Appendix C

This appendix will give you 59 creative ways to implement your bottom line vision. These are not to be legalistic, nor to substitute projects for long term commitments.

Appendix D

No church lives out a perfect A = B commitment. Few live out an A > B commitment to its extreme. In this Appendix, you'll see two churches (both hypothetical) compared side by side in their commitment to world evangelization. View them to see if any characteristics match your church.

Appendix E

This Appendix gives you creative ways to teach children a bottom line vision through new verses to familiar songs.

Appendix F

Destination 2000 has other related materials that you might be interested in. Don't finish this book until you have seen what others materials are available for you, your church, your Sunday School, and your home Bible Study group.

I'm Interested . . .

. . . in possible service with FRONTIERS either at home or abroad.

(Use additional sheets of paper to fill out.)

Name

_____Date_____

Mailing
Address_____City_____St_____ Zip_____

Phone_____Birthdate_____S.S#_____
(Current address valid until: _____)
Permanent
Address_____City_____St_____Zip____

Permanent
Phone_____Citzenship_____

Spouse's name_____Years Married_____

Children's name(s) and birthdates(s)   Marital Status
                                            ☐ Single
_____   ☐ Engaged
                                            ☐ Married   wed. date: _____
_____   ☐ Separated
                                            ☐ Divorded
_____   ☐ Widowed
                                            ☐ Remarried   date: _____

TELL US ABOUT YOURSELF
l. Describe how and when you became a Christian

2. Trace those significant areas of your Christian growth.

3. In what ways and with what success have you helped to bring others to Christ? What further experience have you had discipling new believers?

4. FRONTIERS is committed to working solely among the world's unreached Muslims. My feelings about joining FRONTIERS (Circle one):

   Terrified / Open / Willing / Excited

   Why I'm interested in linking with FRONTIERS:

5. Select the regions of the world that best represents your interests:

   Do you have a burden for any particular country or people group? If so, explain.

   Have you been in touch with any representatives of FRONTIERS? If so explain.

   If considering home staff, what position(s) are you interested in?

6. We are committed to establishing indigenous churches as the goal of all we do. What can you envision yourself doing at home to establish churches among Muslims?

   How could you envision yourself serving in our home office as a part of pre-field preparation?

   What can you envision yourself doing abroad to help establish churches among Muslims?

7. Every missionary with FRONTIERS must have a sending church behind
    them. Which local church will be sending you?

    Church name _____Denomination_____

    Address_____City_____St___Zip_____

    Pastor/Elder/Mission Chairman_____

    Church Phone_____Person to contact\Phone_____

    How long have you taken an active role in this church?

    Give examples of your current involvement.

    To what degree do you think the church may be providing your
    finances?

8. FRONTIERS also believes strongly in working as a team, not as
    individuals. How would you describe yourself as a team player?

    How do you see the role of the team leader?

9. What factors might impact your availability? (For example, family,
    debt, health, other obligations?)

Send To:
Personnel Director
FRONTIERS
P.O. Box 40159
Pasadena, CA 91104
(818) 798-0807

Appendix B

Bottom Line Scriptures

Gen	3:15	Exo	23:09	Deu	24:17-22
Gen	12:1-3	Exo	23:9,12	Deu	26:11-13
Gen	12:10-20	Exo	32:9-13	Deu	27:19
Gen	13:07	Exo	33:1-3,16	Deu	28:10,11,64
Gen	14:13,18-24	Lev	16:29,30	Deu	29:11,22,24-29
Gen	15:1-21	Lev	17:8-10,13,15	Deu	30:1
Gen	17:12,13	Lev	18:26-28	Deu	31:12,16-18
Gen	17:15,16,27	Lev	19:9,10,33,34	Deu	32:7
Gen	18:1-33	Lev	20:2,3	Jos	2:1-24
Gen	20:2-18	Lev	22:17,18	Jos	3:13-17
Gen	21:22,23,25	Lev	23:22	Jos	4:19-24
Gen	22:1-18	Lev	24:16,22	Jos	5:1,14
Gen	23:3-20	Lev	25:23	Jos	6:17,25,27
Gen	24:12-14,26,27	Lev	26:45	Jos	7:09
Gen	24:34-54	Num	9:14	Jos	8:33,35
Gen	26:2-31	Num	10:29-32	Jos	9:1-27
Gen	28:13-15	Num	12:1,2	Jos	11:1-3
Gen	30:27	Num	14:13-19	Jos	13:13
Gen	34:1-31	Num	15:14-16,26	Jos	15:63
Gen	35:5,11,12	Num	19:10	Jos	16:10
Gen	37:5-30,36	Num	22:1-24:25	Jos	17:12,13
Gen	39:1-47:31	Num	32:3,4	Jos	20:09
Exo	2:24	Num	35:15	Jud	1:16,21,28-36
Exo	3:6,8,15-22	Deu	1:04	Jud	2:23-3:5
Exo	4:1-17,22	Deu	2:24-3:11	Jud	3:13,14
Exo	5:1-3,24	Deu	4:6,25-27	Jud	5:24-27
Exo	6:2-8	Deu	5:6-21,32,33	Rut	1:1-4:22
Exo	7:1-11:10	Deu	7:6-9,14	1Sa	4:6-9
Exo	14:4-31	Deu	9:25-29	1Sa	5:1-6:16
Exo	15:14-16,27	Deu	10:14,18,19	1Sa	9:3,6
Exo	17:8-15	Deu	11:25	1Sa	12:22
Exo	18:1,8-12	Deu	14:29	1Sa	17:1-59
Exo	19:5,6	Deu	16:14	1Sa	19:08
Exo	22:21	Deu	23:7,8	1Sa	22:3,4

Destination 2000

1Sa	26:6	2Ch	30:25	Psa	108:1-9
2Sa	7:22-26	2Ch	32:9-23,31	Psa	113:1-9
2Sa	8:1-14	2Ch	36:13,25	Psa	114:7,8
2Sa	10:1-9	Ezr	1:1-7:28	Psa	117:1,2
2Sa	11:6-11	Neh	1:8-6:15	Psa	126:1-3
2Sa	12:29-31	Neh	9:2,10	Psa	137:4-6
2Sa	15:18-22	Neh	10:31	Psa	145:9-13,21
2Sa	21:1-9	Neh	13:16-18	Psa	146:5-10
2Sa	22:44-46,50	Est	1:1-10:3	Psa	148:7-14
2Sa	24:16,18-25	Psa	2:7-12	Psa	150:6
1Ki	3:1-4,11	Psa	7:6-8	Ecl	3:11,14
1Ki	4:20,21,29-34	Psa	8:1-9	Ecl	5:1-7
1Ki	5:1-12	Psa	9:7-12,15-20	Ecl	7:13,14,20
1Ki	8:16,18,19,29	Psa	18:49,50	Ecl	8:13
1Ki	8:41-43,59-61	Psa	23:27-31	Ecl	11:05
1Ki	9:8,9	Psa	24:1-7	Ecl	12:13,14
1Ki	10:1-13,23-25	Psa	25:11	Isa	2:2-4,19
1Ki	11:1-13	Psa	33:8-14	Isa	6:1-13
1Ki	14:21-24,31	Psa	36:7	Isa	7:18-25
1Ki	17:7-18:45	Psa	40:2,3,16	Isa	8:17
1Ki	19:15	Psa	44:11,14	Isa	9:1,2
1Ki	20:1-34	Psa	45:17	Isa	10:20-23
2Ki	1:02	Psa	46:10	Isa	11:9-12
2Ki	3:1-27	Psa	47:1-4,7-9	Isa	13:2-5
2Ki	4:8-37	Psa	48:2,10	Isa	14:01
2Ki	4:42-44	Psa	49:1-20	Isa	16:1-5,11-13
2Ki	5:1-20	Psa	50:1	Isa	17:03
2Ki	6:8-23	Psa	57:5,9-11	Isa	17:6-8
2Ki	8:1,2	Psa	58:10,11	Isa	18:2-7
2Ki	13:20,21	Psa	59:13	Isa	19:1-25
2Ki	15:29,30	Psa	64:9,10	Isa	21:9,10
2Ki	16:9-12	Psa	65:5-8	Isa	23:6-9,17,18
2Ki	17:1-6,23-41	Psa	66:1-20	Isa	24:13-16
2Ki	18:10-12,17-37	Psa	67:1-7	Isa	25:1-8
2Ki	19:10-19,35,36	Psa	68:29-35	Isa	26:9,11,18
2Ki	24:10-17	Psa	69:34-36	Isa	27:5,6
1Ch	2:04	Psa	72:11-15	Isa	29:9-12,18
1Ch	5:23-26	Psa	72:17-19	Isa	30:20-22
1Ch	11:11,12,27-47	Psa	76:11,12	Isa	35:1-10
1Ch	14:17	Psa	77:14	Isa	37:20
1Ch	16:8,14-18	Psa	79:9,10	Isa	40:3-5
1Ch	16:23-31	Psa	82:8	Isa	41:1,17-42:21
1Ch	17:20-24	Psa	83:13-18	Isa	45:5-7,15,16
1Ch	21:15	Psa	86:9,17	Isa	45:21-24
1Ch	22:07	Psa	87:4-6	Isa	48:6-11,18,19
2Ch	2:1-12,17,18	Psa	94:6,7	Isa	49:3,6,7
2Ch	6:13,32,33	Psa	96:1-13	Isa	49:22,23,26
2Ch	8;7,8	Psa	97:1-9	Isa	51:1-6
2Ch	9:1-9,22-24	Psa	98:1-9	Isa	52:9,10,13-15
2Ch	14:9-15	Psa	99:1-5	Isa	55:3-5,8-13
2Ch	17:10,11	Psa	100:1-5	Isa	56:1-8
2Ch	10:1-30	Psa	102:12-22	Isa	59:19
2Ch	26:8	Psa	105:1-4	Isa	60:1-1-16
2Ch	27:9,22,23	Psa	106:8	Isa	61:1-6,9-11

Isa	62:1-6,10-12	Eze	30:1-26	Mat	4:12-25
Isa	63:11-14,17	Eze	32:9-15	Mat	4:12-25
Isa	64:7	Eze	33:29	Mat	5:1-7:28
Isa	65:1,8,9-12	Eze	34:27,30	Mat	8:5-12
Isa	66:8,15-21	Eze	35:3-15	Mat	9:26,31,35-38
Jer	1:4-10	Eze	36:16-36	Mat	10:18
Jer	2:03	Eze	37:13,14	Mat	12:15-21,38-42
Jer	3:17	Eze	37:23-28	Mat	13:11-23,31-50
Jer	4:1,2,15-17	Eze	38:14-23	Mat	15:1-39
Jer	6:18-20	Eze	39:1-8,21-24	Mat	16:13-19
Jer	7:06	Eze	39:27-29	Mat	18:1-19:1
Jer	9:25,26	Eze	44:9	Mat	21:12,13,33-44
Jer	10:6,7	Eze	47:22,23	Mat	22:2-10
Jer	10:10-16,25	Dan	1:1-6/;28	Mat	24:3-14,27-31
Jer	12:14-16	Dan	9:15,18,19	Mat	25:31-46
Jer	13:1-11	Hos	4:6,7	Mat	26:10-13
Jer	14:07	Hos	7:11-16	Mat	28:18-20
Jer	15:02	Hos	8:8-10	Mar	1:2-9,14,15
Jer	16:19-21	Hos	10:10	Mar	1:23-28,38,39
Jer	18:1-10	Hos	11:5,6,8-11	Mar	2:15-17
Jer	22:3,8,9	Hos	14:4-8	Mar	3:7-12
Jer	25:8-38	Joe	2:17-20,30-32	Mar	5:18-20
Jer	26:6	Joe	3:1-17	Mar	6:14
Jer	27:1-11	Amo	1:3-15	Mar	7:14-30
Jer	29:14-18	Amo	2:1-5,9-11	Mar	8:1-10,34-38
Jer	31:3-14	Amo	4:10	Mar	9:01
Jer	32:19-23,27	Amo	9:7,9,11,12	Mar	11:11-18
Jer	33:5-13	Oba	1:1-4,15,16	Mar	12:1-12
Jer	40:1-5	Jon	1:1-4:10	Mar	13:10,27
Jer	44:30	Mic	1:2-2:13	Mar	14:3-9
Jer	49:7-22	Mic	4:2,3,10-15	Mar	15:21
Jer	50:1-7,46	Mic	5:4,5,8,9,15	Mar	16:14-20
Jer	51:1-58	Mic	6:9-16	Luk	3:3-6
Lam	1:18,19,21	Mic	7:10-17	Luk	4:14-19,23-27
Eze	3:5-7	Nah	1:1-3:19	Luk	5:15
Eze	5:5-8,14,15	Hab	2:14	Luk	6:17-19
Eze	6:8-10,13,14	Zep	2:11	Luk	7:1-10,17
Eze	11:16	Zep	3:8-20	Luk	8:4-8,22-39
Eze	12:2,15,16	Hag	2:7,8,20-23	Luk	9:46-56
Eze	14:7,8,21-23	Zec	1:10-21	Luk	10:1-37
Eze	16:1-14,27	Zec	2:10-13	Luk	11:18-32
Eze	16:35-42,59-63	Zec	4:8-14	Luk	13:6-9
Eze	17:1-24	Zec	6:1-8	Luk	14:15-24
Eze	19:4,8,9	Zec	7:10,13,14	Luk	15:1-32
Eze	20:8-14,22-26	Zec	8:9-13,20-23	Luk	17:11-19
Eze	20:44,48	Zec	9:4-7,10	Luk	19:11-27,45,46
Eze	21:2-5	Zec	10:9-12	Luk	20:9-19
Eze	22:4-6	Zec	12:1-9	Luk	21:12-15,24
Eze	22:14-16,29	Zec	13:1-9	Luk	23:26-49
Eze	23:1-48	Zec	14:1-9,16-21	Luk	24:45-48
Eze	24:25-27	Mal	1:4,5,10,11,14	Joh	1:1-18,29
Eze	25:1-26:6	Mal	3:16	Joh	2:13-17
Eze	28:20-29:9	Mat	1:3,5,6	Joh	3:12-21,31-36
Eze	29:12-16	Mat	3:1-12	Joh	4:1-54

Joh	5:19-31	Act	27:1,2	Php	2:6-11	
Joh	6:35-40,44-58	Act	27:21-28:10	Col	1:6,16-20,23-29	
Joh	7:36	Act	28:23-31	Col	2:9-15	
Joh	8:12,25	Rom	1:1-6,8	Col	3:2-6	
Joh	9:05	Rom	1:13-16,18-32	1Th	1:2-10	
Joh	10:1-18	Rom	2:1-29	1Th	2:15-20	
Joh	11:25-27,47,48	Rom	3:6,9-31	1Th	5:1-11	
Joh	11:51,52	Rom	4:9-25	2Th	1:3-12	
Joh	12:19	Rom	5:6-21	2Th	2:11,12	
Joh	12:20-33,37-40	Rom	8:18-23	1Ti	2:1-8	
Joh	13:20,35	Rom	9:1-33	1Ti	3:16	
Joh	14:15-31	Rom	10:4,11-20	1Ti	4:9,10	
Joh	15:18-27	Rom	11:1-36	2Ti	4:1-4,17	
Joh	16:5-11	Rom	15:7-33	Tit	2:11-14	
Joh	17:1-26	Rom	16:25	Heb	1:1-3;6	
Joh	18:33-37	1Co	1:18-25	Heb	5:8-10	
Joh	19:19-21	1Co	3:5-9	Heb	6:13-19	
Joh	20:21-23	1Co	3:21-4:17	Heb	7:23-27	
Act	1:1-10	1Co	6:9-11	Heb	8:1-2,6	
Act	2:1-41	1Co	7:17-24	Heb	9:11-15,23-28	
Act	3:11-26	1Co	8:5,6	Heb	11:8-19	
Act	4:16,23-25	1Co	9:16-27	Jam	1:1	
Act	6:1-7	1Co	10:31,32	1Pe	1:1,2	
Act	7:1-8:14	1Co	12:4-6,12,13	1Pe	2:9-12	
Act	8:25-9:16	1Co	15:20-28	1Pe	3:18-22	
Act	10:1-11:30	2Co	2:12-3:3	2Pe	3:5-12	
Act	13:1-4,6-12,16	2Co	4:3,4,6	1Jo	3:08	
Act	13:26,40-52	2Co	5:14-21	1Jo	4:9-14	
Act	14:1,15-17	2Co	10:13-16	Jud	0:00	
Act	14:26-15:35	Gal	1:4,5,15-17	Rev	1:4-8	
Act	16:1-10,16-40	Gal	2:1-17	Rev	2:26-27	
Act	17:4,10-12	Gal	3:8,9,14,16	Rev	3:10	
Act	17:16-34	Gal	3:21-29	Rev	4:1-7:17	
Act	18:6-8	Gal	6:14	Rev	8:6-10:11	
Act	19:17-20	Eph	1:3-23	Rev	11:15-19	
Act	20:21	Eph	2:11-3:12	Rev	13:1-15:8	
Act	21:19	Eph	4:4-6,20-24	Rev	17:13-18	
Act	22:21	Eph	6:19,20	Rev	18:1-3	
Act	26:1-30	Php	1:2-11	Rev	19:1-16	

| Appendix C |

What Now?
59 Action Steps
for You & Your Church

You've caught a vision of God's heart for the nations. And you want to get into action. You desperately want to do something after you've been exposed to what God is up to in His Word and in His works.

We'll list some possible action steps. But first a word of caution. These action steps are not to be a "compartment" of your life which you 'dabble in' every now and then. Don't allow them to be seen as one time events—which is easy to do. Rather, see them as tools to help you integrate a world vision into your everyday life. The two should be inseperable.

Build and Act on the Vision:
A To-Do List

Individual Action Steps

Commit Yourself
1. Write a letter to a distant best friend telling of your commitment to the vision of God's great purpose on earth.
2. List your topline blessings and pray/meditate on how you can consecrate each one as a bottom line blessing.

Your life is a big "reception": What do you have that
you have not received? How can these blessings be channeled
into God's unchangeable purpose?
　　　—spiritual　gifts
　　　—ethnic　heritage
　　　—big-even "negative"-events that have shaped you
　　　—education
　　　—family　traditions
　　　—physical　skills,　talents
　　　—supportive　friends
3.　Sign the "Caleb Declaration" of commitment:
"Then Caleb quieted the people before Moses and said,
'We should by all means go up and take possession of
it, for we shall surely overcome it'" (Numbers 13:30).
By the grace of God and for His glory, I commit my entire
life to obeying His commission of Matthew 28:18-20, wherever and however He leads me, giving priority to the
peoples currently beyond the reach of the Gospel (Romans
15:20-21).
As an expression of my commitment, I will attempt to
fulfill the following:
　　1. I will go to another culture or stay in this one,
　　　　depending on the Lord's leading.
　　2. I will share my vision with other Christians, recognizing
　　　　that my local church or campus student group are
　　　　the obvious places for me to begin.
　　3. As others grow in commitment ot Christ's global
　　　　cause, I will trust that three of them will sign the
　　　　Caleb Declaration.
　　4. To help me follow through with my commitment,
　　　　I will "report" to someone—perhaps my pastor—
　　　　monthly on how I am building and acting on this
　　　　vision to reach every nation.

Signature_____
Date_____

(Consider photocopying this declaration and posting it where you'll see it often.)

4. Explore your role as a "priest" (1Peter 2:9-10). What does a priest do? How can you literally or figuratively perform those services for the unreached peoples of the world? The consecration rites of the sons of Aaron lasted seven days. What could you do daily for a week that would cement in your memory the fact that you are one of a people of God's own possession, a holy nation, a kingdom of priests?

5. List activities you can do away with to better commit your time to God's purpose.

6. Raise an "Ebenezer" (1 Sam. 7:12): Actually build a monument (a pile of stones? a plaque? a slab of wet concrete?) to acknowledge your determination to align your life with God's unchangeable purpose; then annually spend a full day commemorating and renewing your commitment.

7. If there is a possibility of your going to the field, ask around for a mission mentor you can be accountable to. Ask locally first, then check with your denomination. Finally, a national tracking and advising system operated by Caleb Project (1605 Elizabeth St., Pasadena, CA 91104 USA) will encourage you to progress in your commitment levels.

Share

8. Compile your list of topline blessings (see under Commitment #2, pg 213) and ask others for clues as to other blessings you're not realizing in your life. You'll then have to explain the "blessed to be a blessing" principle!

9. Find one or two friends who will meet with you for a regular (weekly? bi-weekly? monthly?) unreached peoples prayer session. As you develop as a small group: A) Help each other clarify your motives in mission-interest. B)

Hold each other accountable for Bible study, prayer and giving. C) Encourage each other with global breakthroughs. 10. Set up a monthly global awareness booktable in your church narthex once a month. Set out pamphlets from your church's mission organizations, video and audio tapes and study books to encourage others to catch the vision. Compile your own materials or contact William Carey Library (1705 N. Sierra Bonita Av, Pasadena, CA 91104) for information on a pre-packaged library of materials called a *World Christian Display Table.*

Pray

11. Set up a "Nation's Prayer Reminder" system, perhaps as simple as a card with one an unreached people group listed, to remind you to pray while you are doing dishes, taking a shower, jogging, etc.

12. Put a sticky label-dot on your watch, your clock at home or work and/or your car's rearview mirror to remind you to pray for the Lord of the harvest to thrust forth laborers.

13. Adopt a specific team overseas to pray for in the Muslim, Buddhist, Hindu, Tribal, or Chinese world. Contact FRONTIERS for a specific Muslim team.

14. Subscribe to the Global Prayer Digest. This monthly prayer guide features an unreached people group each day. You can join with thousands of other prayer warriors focusing on that group, that day. Send for a sample or subscribe for $6 from Global Prayer Digest Subscriptions, 1605 Elizabeth St., Pasadena, CA 91104 USA.

15. Get the book *Operation World*: A day-to-day guide to praying for the world by Patrick Johnstone to further guide your prayers for the unreached peoples of the earth. Order from your local Christian bookstore or through Destination 2000, PO Box 40159, Pasadena, CA 91104.

16. Beginning with those profiled in this book, pray over a list of unreached peoples. Once a month pray for them

all at once, finding their locations on a world map. Perhaps "tithe" a Sunday and spend one-tenth of your day in prayer for the nations.

17.   Attend a "Concert of Prayer" with your family or a group of friends. These area-wide prayer gatherings concentrate on revival, leading to "fullness"—God's blessing on us His people, and "fulfillment"—His blessing on every people. Contact the US national office of Concerts of Prayer for locations near you: Concerts of Prayer, Pentagon Powers 4550 W. 77th Suite #220 Minneapolis, MN 55435.

Study
18.   Review your understanding of the vision of "A Church for Every People by the Year 2000." Begin to memorize some of the focal passages cited in this study.

19.   Evaluate the highlighted passages in your personal study Bible—how many of the passages refer to God's blessing the nations (bottom line) and how many refer to God's blessing you (top line)?

20.   Buy a new Bible and underline the passages that specifically refer to the bottom line—God's blessing for the nations.

21. Take the "Perspectives on the World Christian Movement" course which extensively covers the biblical, historical, cultural and strategic aspects of God's plan to reach every people, tribe, tongue and nation. Extension classes are offered throughout the world, and the course can be taken by correspondence. Contact the Perspectives Study Program, 1605 Elizabeth St., Pasadena, CA 91104 USA.

22.   Subscribe to a dozen or more mission magazines and newsletters. Some of the generic "must-reads" include:

Mission Frontiers, Records Office, 1605 Elizabeth St., Pasadena CA 91104 USA.

Evangelical Missions Quarterly, Box 794, Wheaton IL 60189 USA.

Pulse, Box 794, Wheaton IL 60189 USA.

23. Read your Sunday newspaper and a national or large metropolitan Sunday newspaper and notice:
—The hot spots of the news around the world. How could God be using this incident to further His unchangeable plan to bless the nations?
—Any mention of unreached people groups. What is God doing among them even through problems and the wrath of men to accomplish His great purpose? Determine how much time you'll devote weekly to think through world news relating to unreached people groups.
24. Study what is happening in North American business abroad. Be aware of what North America is exporting, think through how that is affecting the nations and pray accordingly.
25. Study the book *Serve As A Sender*, a surprising, step-by-step approach to being a fully equipped sender to your missionaries. Order from Emmaus Road International, 7150 Tanner Court, San Diego, CA 92111 (619/292-7020).
26. Compile a cassette library of missiological tapes that focus on the biblical, historical, cultural and strategic factors of finishing the task of the Great Commission. As if you're on a self-study course and are cramming for a final exam, listen to these tapes while driving, jogging or doing house or yard work. Such tapes are available from William Carey Library, Box 40129, Pasadena, CA 91114 USA. Ask for a resource catalog listing audio and video titles.
27. Read and jot findings in books that focus on un-reached peoples and finishing the task. An excellent basic library of these types of books is called *The World Christian Bookshelf*, with twelve basic books to study. Write or phone William Carey Library (818/798-0819 1705 N. Sierra Bonita, Av. Pasadena, CA 91104).
28. Go to school. For information on schools offering various mission training programs, send for a copy of this year's "Great Commission Handbook" (SMS Publications, 1418 Lake St., Evanston, IL 60201 USA; 708/328-

3386) or the "Evangelical Missions Quarterly Guide to Continuing Education" (Box 794, Wheaton IL 60189 USA).

Align Your Lifestyle

29. Evaluate the Christian records and books you own. How many of them are about God blessing you in top line blessings? How many incorporate bottom line topics? Work toward a balance in the input you and your family get from the music and literature in your home.
30. Shop carefully for any item. Find the lowest price and give away what you saved!
31. Collect your loose change daily, count it monthly and deposit it. Then send a check for that amount to an unreached peoples project championed by your mission agency.
32. Find out the average salary of a minister in your denomination. If it is lower than your salary, adjust to it over a period of months or years. Perhaps cut $100 out of your budget each month or every two months until your level of living matches that average ministerial salary. Give what you save to your selected unreached peoples mission effort!
33. Consult a financial planner and get help setting a specific plan to decrease debt and increase your giving to the frontier mission efforts of your church or mission agency.

Give Time

34. Write to missionaries working on the front lines. Get personal in your news of the homefront. Send Sunday funny papers. Encourage. Don't expect an answer. Be cautious in writing any missionary working in restricted-access countries (Check with your mission agency for guidelines).
35. Connect with a mission agency wanting to learn more about a particular unreached group and clip newspaper and magazine references about that people and its

geographical area.

36. Volunteer five hours weekly to your church or mission agency in some effort to reach unreached peoples, regardless of how indirectly.

37. Visit your nearest Christian radio station and encourage them to air mission programs about unreached people groups. Some "generic" mission programs, which don't request funds, include: "Around the World" with NewService 2000; "World Prayer 2000" with Jack McAllister, and *Global Prayer Digest* Radio Spots sponsored by Far East Broadcasting Corporation's Mission Vision Network, Box 1, La Mirada, Ca 90637 USA.

38. Volunteer to help in a local or regional international student ministry. Shock foreign students by being interested in, not only what political country they are from, but what people they are from. If you find students who are from people groups who have no strong Christian witness, relay this information to the international student organization headquarters, your mission agency and the Adopt-A-People Clearinghouse (1539 E. Howard St., Pasadena CA 90114 USA).

You just may be hosting an international student who could be the first one of his or her people to come to Christ. Mission groups targeting that people group will be more than interested to follow up on that individual, as he or she could be helpful to teach language nuances, customs and other valuable 'inside' information. And, perhaps that one student will be the key, the evangelist who will plant a church and foster a movement to Christ in his or her own people group!

39. Find out if there are internationals from unreached people groups working or living in your community. Remember that individuals from most Muslim, Hindu and Buddhist people will be from unreached groups. Start up relationships with these internationals, realizing again that they may be precisely the one family God has ordained

to carry the Gospel back to their homeland! Contact "Doorstep Opportunities" for ideas on how to best minister cross-culturally in your area; write Doorstep Opportunities, 1605 Elizabeth St., Pasadena, CA 91104 USA.

40. Use your vacation time here or overseas to help research an unreached people group or assist in pre-evangelism (relief work, literature distribution, etc.) in a major city with unreached people communities. Contact your unreached peoples- focused mission agency for opportunities. Get a clear idea of short-terming opportunities in "Stepping Out: A Guide to Short-Term Missions" available through William Carey Library, address above.

41. Help with research. Link up with your mission agency or a group such as the "Adopt-A-People Clearinghouse" (1539 E. Howard St., Pasadena CA 91104 USA) and find out what needs to be found out about a particular people group. You'll be amazed at how much strategic research needed by the mission community has already been done in decades' worth of sociological and anthropological studies, just sitting in your nearest university library!

42. Draw a time-line of your life from birth to death. Consider tithing a tenth of your "expected" lifetime to be involved fulltime in sending or giving.

43. Contact a mission agency targeting unreached peoples and start corresponding about possible short-term and career assignments.

44. Research the possibilities of becoming a part-time or fulltime mission mobilizer in your area. Learn how to share the vision with groups. Encourage prayer, giving and activism on behalf of the unreached. Contact your mission agency for ideas. Or, to become a "generic" mission mobilizer representing all evangelical mission groups, write Regional Office Coordinator of the US Center for World Mission for information on serving in your area. Also, the Mobilization Division of the US Center for World Mission can equip you with materials to encourage churches to

"adopt" and unreached people group. Write and ask for an Adopt-A-People Advocate Kit. The US Center address is 1605 Elizabeth St., Pasadena, CA 91104 USA.

Action Steps for Your Fellowship Group or Church

Work with others, particularly the leadership of your church or fellowship group, to initiate the following educational steps in your group. Each of these resources is available through the US Center for World Mission or a cooperating mission organization. (For information on resources, contact the Mobilization Division, US Center for World Mission, 1605 Elizabeth St., Pasadena, CA 91104 USA.)

45. Post Unreached Peoples Posters around your facility. These striking posters map out the details of the remaining task of reaching every people group for Christ.

46. Set out "Catch the Vision" brochures. These comprehensive pamphlets overview the biblical and strategic vision of finishing the task of the Great Commission. (Available in 10-packs through the U.S. Center for World Missions.)

47. Host a "Vision for the Nations" Sunday. This is a one-Sunday mission emphasis on the challenge of planting a church among each of the remaining unreached people groups. The packet includes Sunday School lessons for all ages, sermon outlines and samples, bulletin inserts for note-taking and responses, a small group Bible study guide on unreached peoples and take-home prayer guides for the family. A stunning one-day mission emphasis!

48. Use the "Catch the Vision 2000" study course in adult Sunday School, in home-group Bible studies, at midweek services, or in Sunday evening sessions. The complete 12-session curriculum manual is available through William Carey Library, Box 40129, Pasadena, CA 91114 USA.

49. For an even more intensive study of God's unchange-

able purpose to bless every people with His offer of salvation, study through the video-based course of Destination 2000 available through FRONTIERS, P.O. Box 40159 Pasadena, CA 91104.

50. Since, as a group, you're getting out of the pew and into the battlefield, study through the nine-session video course Spiritual Warfare available through Emmaus Road International, 7150 Tanner Court, San Diego, CA 92111 (619/292-7020).

51. Initiate a monthly mission fellowship in your church to study the implications of the biblical, historical, cultural and strategic aspects of God's global purpose. The "Year of Vision" is a perfect program that provides video-based teaching guides for group discussion, instructions on how to pray daily for unreached peoples and a plan for actually "adopting" an unreached people group. These twelve 90-minute sessions form an entire year's worth of mission education!

52. As a church, study your church's mission efforts:

   A) How can you better pray for and equip your missionaries to reached peoples to encourage nationals to become sending churches—sending their own missionaries to unreached peoples?

   B.) How can you better pray for and equip your missionaries working among unreached groups?

   C.) List all your missionaries and their locations on a sheet of paper and memorize them.

53. Begin to amplify and expand on your fellowship's mission educational foundation by hosting incisive seminars on various aspects of reaching the unreached. Some basic seminars—ideal for inviting others to catch the foundational vision of God's global plan-include:

   —Catch the Vision 2000 Seminar
   —Destination 2000 Seminar
   —A Mini-Perspectives Seminar

Other more specific aspects of what God is doing today

are presented in specialized seminars including:
>   —Muslim Awareness Seminars
>   —China Awareness Seminars
>   —An Introduction to Cross-Cultural Ministry Seminars

nars
>   —"Nothing Good Just Happens": 3-Day Cross-Cultural Ministry Training for Church Leadership.

For information on booking any of the above seminars, contact the US Center for World Mission Mobilization Division, 1605 Elizabeth St., Pasadena, CA 91104 who will put you in touch with the organizations offering each.

54.   Initiate the strategies and planning you will find in special handbooks from the Association of Church Missions Committees (ACMC) Box ACMC, Wheaton, IL 60189-8000. Some of these include "Your Church Missions Policy Handbook", "Cultivating a Missions-Active Church" and "Missions Conference Planner". For ongoing help in mobilizing your church, consider joining ACMC or the Association of International Mission Services organization for charismatically-oriented congregations (AIMS, Box 60534, Virginia Beach, VA 23464 USA).

55.   Take specific steps to link with a mission agency targeting a specific people group; "adopt" a people! The varying degrees of responsibility your church can assume in this demanding enterprise are determined by you as a church and the agency. Contact your unreached-people-targeting mission agency or the Adopt-A-People Clearinghouse, 1539 E. Howard St., Pasadena, CA 91104, for ideas on how to adopt an unreached group.

56.   Send your pastor(s) to the field. Nothing will infuse church leadership with a vision to help complete the Great Commission as a firsthand experience in researching or engaging an unreached group.

57.   Second your pastor or other church leader to a mission agency, perhaps even to do clerical work! Nothing will help your church leadership sympathize more with the

demands of mission work than seeing the support system operations at agency headquarters.

58. Send your pastor to the "Perspectives on the World Christian Movement" intensive course held each January on the campus of the US Center for World Mission in Pasadena, California. Contact the Perspectives Study Course offices at 1605 Elizabeth St., Pasadena, CA 91104 for details, or for the location of the Perspectives extension course offered nearest you.

59. Hold a garage sale and give the money away to a mission agency working among a people not yet reached.

Enough ideas to prod your thinking? Your own response to the vision of God's orchestration of world events to proclaim His character to every people, tribe, tongue and nation, might never appear on such an action-step list. But since to whom much is given, much is required, your sense of that vision demands your response. What will you do?

If nothing else, do the foundational action step. Since you've had a chance to "look to the fields," get good at the basic response Jesus commanded: "Beseech the Lord of the harvest to send out workers into His harvest" (Matthew 9:38). Pray!

(Prepared by Bill Stearns of the US Center for World Mission.)

Characteristics of Two Extreme Churches

A > B	A = B
Missions is seen as a one week event.	World Evanglelization is in every aspect of the church throughout the year.
Only those who are "Holy" or "Called" get involved	Everyone has a role in evangelizing the world.
Missions is rarely mentioned in sermons outisde of missions week.	God's heart for the nations is heard in almost every sermon.
Adults decide on their own if God is "Calling" them into missions.	Church leadership challenges couples and singles to consider going overseas.
I'ts 'O.K.' if you want to go overseas short term.	Short terms are not only encouraged but developed from within the Church.
The terms 'people groups' or 'unreached peoples' are foreign to the average layperson.	Sunday School children are familiar with the terms 'unreached peoples' or 'people groups'.

A > B	A = B
The average attender can only name 2 or 3 verses that deals with missions.	The average layperson can name hundreds of verses, knowing God's heart for all nations is the theme of the Bible.
The idea of adopting a people group is foreign to them.	They are prayerfully considering or have already adopted a people group.
The first thing dropped in the Church's budget is missions.	The Pastor won't take a paycheck until all missionaries are paid.
Most members don't know who their missionaries are or where they're serving.	Most know who the Church missionaries are, where they serve, and what their needs are.
Mission prayer meetings aren't usually held, and are poorly attended when held.	Mission prayer meetings are held consistently, well attended, and they join in on "Concerts of Prayer."
Few are even aware of the course "Perspectives On A World Christian Movement."	Many have taken Perspectives already and are encouraging others to do the same.
Missions and missionaries get as little money as possible.	The Church is hoping to give 50% of their budget to missions.
Missions, though never stated, in reality is seen as a 'necessary evil.'	World Evangelization is half the reason the Church exists.

Creative Bottom Line Verses . . .

THE B-I-B-L-E

The B-I-B-L-E
It has one story you see,
To reach all nations with God's love
the B-I-B-L-E

JESUS LOVES THE LITTLE CHILDREN

Jesus loves the unreached children,
All the unreached children of the world.
Muslims,Buddhists, Hin-dus,Chinese,
Tribals need Him too.
Jesus died for all the children of the world.

IF YOU'RE BLESSED TO BE A BLESSING

If you're blessed to be a blessing, clap your hands (2X)
If you're blessed to be a blessing,
then your life will surely show it.
If you're blessed to be a blessing, clap your hands.

. . . To Familiar Children's Songs.

JESUS LOVES ME

Jesus loves the nations
Every tongue and every tribe
He wants to use you
To reach them to be His Bride.

Yes, Jesus loves them, (3X)
For the Bible tells me so.

OUR GOD IS AN AWESOME GOD

Our God is a faithful God
He keeps His promises
To reach all nations
Our God is a faithful God.

A.D.
Moving the Church into the 21st Century

Is now available in . . .

Video and Audio

Ten one-half hour videos bring the message to life over a period of 12 weeks for your own enrichment, your Sunday School class, or your home Bible Study. It is for rent or purchase. Audio is available for purchase as well.

or

Live!

For your Church or School
by one of our trained speakers.

also available is the

Children's Version of Destination 2000

when you host the adult seminar.

If you're looking for more depth into God's word, consider getting ***Destination 2000's Follow-up Book***. This book, the video series, and the live seminar are limited in the amount of material they can cover. The follow-up book goes deeper.

Not only does it give different material to review the lessons learned through Destination 2000, but it also gives you a more in-depth view of the 'Story of the Bible.'

It covers such topics as Abraham's ordeal in sacrificing Isaac, 'Final Judgment' versus 'Corrective Judgment', 'Specific Revelation' versus 'General Revelation', and other subject matter which will give you a firmer grasp in understanding of God's word and His commitment to reach people from every tongue, tribe, and nation.

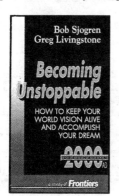

In ***Becoming Unstoppable,*** Bob Sjogren and Greg Livingstone offer practical ways to keep your world vision and fulfill your dream from their own personal experience.

They address such issues as:
- How do you keep your world vision?
- When are you sure you're 'called'?
- What really qualifies you to be a missionary?
- What makes a good 'sender'?
- What about parents that don't want you to go?
- What should I do about my singleness?
- What should I do to preprare for the field?

Let their lives encourage you as you seek to fulfill your dream of being a blessing to the nations.

> For more information regarding the books, the video, or the seminar, write to Destination 2000
> c/o FRONTIERS, PO Box 40159 Pasadena, CA 91104

Destination 2000 Order Form

(Photo copy this so you may have it for further use.)

T-Shirts and Sweatshirts:

T-Shirts   (Circle One)

Size:	M L Ex-L		
Price:	$10		_____
Picture:	Tennis Player Avant-Garde		
Postage:	1st Class $1.85		_____

Subtotal #1 _____

Sweatshirts

Size:	M L Ex-L		
Price	$15		_____
Picture:	Tennis Player or Avant-Garde		
Postage:	1st Class $2.40		_____

Books/Pictures:

Subtotal #2 _____

Destination 2000	~~$6.95~~	$5.00	_____
Becoming Unstoppable	~~$6.95~~	$5.00	_____
Destination 2000 Follow-Up Book		$6.95	_____
Postage: Add $1.50 for 1st bk, $0.50 for addn. bks			_____
Pictures: (Circle one) Tennis or A-G		$1.00	_____

Video/Audio Series:

Subtotal #3 _____

Destination 2000 in Video and Audio Series

Suggested Retail Price: V:$100   A:$25   _____

or "Whatever you can afford" (Write in for more information.)

Rental of Video Series: $20 per month   _____

Subtotal #4 _____

_____	Subtotal #1
_____	Subtotal #2
_____	Subtotal #3
_____	Subtotal #4

(Allow 4-6 weeks for delivery)

_____ **California Residents** add 6.75% Sales Tax

_____ Grand Total   (Make All Checks Payable To: FRONTIERS)

Mail To:

Name: _____

Address: _____

City/State/Zip _____

Telephone: (__) —

Please Print Clearly!

Send To: Destination 2000 c/o FRONTIERS
P.O. Box 40159 Pasadena, CA 91104 (818) 798-0807